Skills Practice

Workbook

Grade 3

Bothell, WA • Chicago, IL • Columbus, OH • New York, NY

MHEonline.com

Send all inquiries to:
McGraw-Hill Education
8787 Orion Place
Columbus, OH 43240

ISBN: 978-0-07-668507-3
MHID: 0-07-668507-1

Printed in the United States of America.

5 6 7 8 9 10 LHS 23 22 21 20

Table of Contents

Unit 2

Unit 3

Unit 4

Unit 5

Unit 6

Spellings for the /ā/, /ī/, and /ō/ Sounds

FOCUS
- /ā/ can be spelled a and a_e.
  Examples: _a_corn, inv_a_d_e_
- /ī/ can be spelled i and i_e.
  Examples: _i_ron, emp_i_r_e_
- /ō/ can be spelled o and o_e.
  Examples: m_o_ment, aw_o_k_e_

PRACTICE Circle the word in each pair with the correct /ā/, /ī/, or /ō/ spelling.

1.	faiver	favor
2.	lone	loane
3.	beside	bisyde
4.	wyldiest	wildest
5.	updait	update
6.	coeld	cold
7.	basic	baisic
8.	aleyve	alive
9.	plate	playt
10.	teluscoap	telescope

APPLY Choose a word from each pair that completes
the sentence and contains an /ā/, /ī/, or /ō/ sound.
Write the word on the line.

11. We heard a new song on the _____. (radio, dashboard)

12. Ms. Andrews asked us to _____ the book's characters. (answer, describe)

13. I respect my grandfather, and he is my _____. (friend, idol)

14. The holiday _____ included floats and a marching band. (party, parade)

15. The unpleasant _____ came from the basement. (odor, smell)

16. I intend to _____ a fort in the backyard. (create, explore)

17. Maya wants to _____ ten people to her party. (invite, compose)

18. My aunt got married one _____ ago today. (decade, month)

19. It was snowing very hard, so we stopped at a _____. (gateway, hotel)

20. The _____ of grass grew quickly along the fence posts. (blades, pony)

Phonics • *Skills Practice*

Compound Words

> **FOCUS** A **compound word** is one word that has two smaller words in it.
>
> **bird + house = birdhouse** *"a house for a bird"*
> A compound word can have the same meaning as the two words in it, as in *birdhouse*, or it can have a new meaning.
> **cow + boy = cowboy** *"a male who herds cattle"*
>   (not *"a boy who is a cow"*)

PRACTICE Circle the compound word in each sentence. Then look closely at the two words that make up each compound word. Write *same meaning* or *new meaning* on the line.

1. Ariana grabbed a strawberry from the refrigerator. _____

2. I enjoy taking afternoon walks when the weather is warm.
   _____

3. My older brother just became a homeowner._____

4. The cheerleader tried to get the crowd to be more spirited.
   _____

5. Judge Anders studied the information filed in the lawsuit.
   _____

6. The library brings in a storyteller every Wednesday.
   _____

7. My friend's grandmother is a famous musician._____

8. We celebrated Tyson's birthday by going to the park.
   _____

APPLY Create a compound word from the two words provided. Fill in the blanks to define the new compound words.

9. head + band = _____

"a _____ worn on the _____"

10. sun + shine = _____

"the _____ of the bright _____"

11. gold + fish = _____

"a _____ -colored _____"

Look at the compound words in the box and read the definitions below the box. Then write the correct word from the box on the line next to each compound word's definition.

skyscraper	headache	notebook	sweetheart

12. "a pain felt in the head" _____

13. "a kind or nice person" _____

14. "a book used to write or record notes or ideas" _____

15. "a very tall building" _____

Word Analysis • *Skills Practice*

Fluency Checklist

As you read the following passage, be sure to keep these things in mind to help you read with the appropriate rate, accuracy, and expression.

As you read, make sure you

☐ pause longer at a period or other ending punctuation.

☐ raise your voice at a question mark.

☐ use expression when you come to an exclamation point.

☐ pause at commas but not as long as you would at a period.

☐ think of the character and how he or she might say his or her words whenever you come to quotation marks.

☐ remember not to read so fast that someone listening could not hear the individual words or make sense of what is being read.

☐ stop and reread something that does not make sense.

A Woman of Action

Jane Addams was never happy on the sidelines of life. In the 1880s, America was changing. People from many different countries were arriving in the cities, and many of them were poor or jobless. Addams could not ignore the needs of these people. She was a person who stood up for the rights of many.

Women did not have many choices in life back then. At that time, most women were expected to get married and raise a family. Addams chose not to follow that path. Her father taught her to listen to her heart and act on her beliefs. Addams found a different purpose for her life.

She could not ignore the poverty and despair around her. Thousands of people lived in low-quality housing. They did not have enough food to eat. Many could not get good medical care. Addams helped those people. She opened a community center, improved education, and worked to pass laws to protect children.

At a time when women were not world leaders, Addams was an exception. She acted on her beliefs and found ways to help others. By starting programs to help the poor, she earned a place in history. Jane Addams was a remarkable woman of action.

Spellings for the /ē/ and /ū/ Sounds

FOCUS
- /ē/ can be spelled e and e_e.
  Examples: *become, complete*
- /ū/ can be spelled u and u_e.
  Examples: *argument, accuse*

PRACTICE Read each word below. Circle *Yes* if the word has the /ē/ or /ū/ sound. Circle *No* if the word does not have either sound.

1. dispute	Yes	No
2. broken	Yes	No
3. frustrated	Yes	No
4. impede	Yes	No
5. unicorn	Yes	No
6. weather	Yes	No
7. meter	Yes	No
8. element	Yes	No
9. uncle	Yes	No
10. tribute	Yes	No

APPLY Write a word from the box to complete each sentence. Below the sentence, write the word on the line and circle the correct /ē/ or /ū/ sound and the spelling the word contains.

| perfume | prevent | abuse | elect | unite | Chinese |

11. Animal _____ is a serious crime.

_____ has the (/ē/, /ū/) sound spelled (e, e_e, u, u_e).

12. People who live in a specific Southeast Asian country are _____.

_____ has the (/ē/, /ū/) sound spelled (e, e_e, u, u_e).

13. To _____ is to be part of a group of people that have joined together.

_____ has the (/ē/, /ū/) sound spelled (e, e_e, u, u_e).

14. Voters have the right to _____ lawmakers in their region.

_____ has the (/ē/, /ū/) sound spelled (e, e_e, u, u_e).

15. I bought a light, floral-scented _____.

_____ has the (/ē/, /ū/) sound spelled (e, e_e, u, u_e).

16. You can _____ some illnesses by eating healthful foods and exercising regularly.

_____ has the (/ē/, /ū/) sound spelled (e, e_e, u, u_e).

Phonics • *Skills Practice*

Antonyms and Synonyms

> **_FOCUS_** **Antonyms** are words that have opposite meanings. **Synonyms** are words with the same or nearly the same meanings. A dictionary or thesaurus can help you find synonyms for words. Sometimes a dictionary or thesaurus also lists antonyms.
>
> Example: _happy_
>
> Antonyms for _happy_: sorrowful, unhappy
>
> Synonyms for _happy_: cheerful, glad

PRACTICE **For each word provided, circle an antonym of that word.**

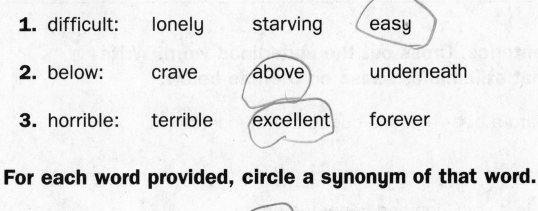

1. difficult: lonely   starving   (easy)

2. below: crave   (above)   underneath

3. horrible: terrible   (excellent)   forever

For each word provided, circle a synonym of that word.

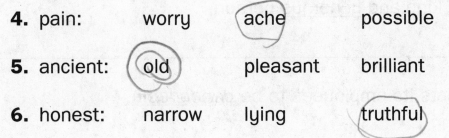

4. pain: worry   (ache)   possible

5. ancient: (old)   pleasant   brilliant

6. honest: narrow   lying   (truthful)

APPLY Read each sentence. Cross out the underlined word. Write an antonym that makes more sense on the line below.

7. Chris felt unprepared and ~~calm~~ as he studied for his science test.

_____

8. The ~~cheap~~ cell phone cost too much money.

_____

9. Which ~~answers~~ do you want to ask the teacher?

_____

10. The ~~quiet~~ crowd screamed and cheered.

_____

Read each sentence. Cross out the underlined word. Write a synonym that still makes sense on the line below.

11. Carlos heard a ~~bizarre~~ sound during the thunderstorm.

_____

12. My sister is a very kind and ~~generous~~ person.

_____

13. The company expects its employees to be ~~dependable~~.

_____

14. The dress Kaitlyn will wear to her wedding is ~~gorgeous~~.

_____

Word Analysis • *Skills Practice*

Fluency Checklist

As you read the following passage, be sure to keep these things in mind to help you read with the appropriate rate, accuracy, and expression.

As you read, make sure you

☐ pause longer at a period or other ending punctuation.

☐ raise your voice at a question mark.

☐ use expression when you come to an exclamation point.

☐ pause at commas but not as long as you would at a period.

☐ think of the character and how he or she might say his or her words whenever you come to quotation marks.

☐ remember not to read so fast that someone listening could not hear the individual words or make sense of what is being read.

☐ stop and reread something that does not make sense.

Community Pride

An excited buzz went through the room. The class was discussing their community mural project. They had to plan a design. The mural needed to show how they felt about their town. Their teacher, Ms. Sanchez, asked what the mural should include.

"Native Americans lived here first," said Katie. "We should show their pueblos and crops."

"What about pioneers?" asked Van. "They sacrificed a lot to come here. They built this town."

"We should add in desert plants and animals," said Tanya. "We live in the desert, and these living things are our neighbors too." Soon there was a very long list on the paper.

"I think we need one big idea to pull our mural together," said Ms. Sanchez. "It should include everything we have been discussing."

The students knew that their community was diverse. People from many different cultures lived and worked together. All kinds of backgrounds were what made the community work.

"Our mural should celebrate all the people who make a contribution," said Jeff.

"Our town's history and diverse culture should shine through in the scenes on the mural," said Tanya.

The class agreed. They began planning. The mural would weave the past, present, and future together. It would also be full of every kind of life in the community. It would show the respect they had for their community. And it would show the joy they felt to be part of such a unique place.

Spellings for the /j/ and /s/ Sounds

FOCUS
- /j/ can be spelled *ge* and *gi_*.
  Examples: *le<u>ge</u>nd, ma<u>gi</u>c*
- /**s**/ can be spelled *ce*, *ci_*, and *cy*.
  Examples: *noti<u>ce</u>, pre<u>ci</u>se*, and *spi<u>cy</u>*

PRACTICE Read each word. Write *Yes* if it has one of the /j/ or /s/ spellings shown in the Focus box above. Write *No* if it does not. If you answered *Yes* to a word, circle the letters in the word that spell the /j/ or /s/ sound from the Focus box.

1. giraffe   _____

2. calendar   _____

3. recite   _____

4. getting   _____

5. vacancy   _____

6. cringe   _____

7. emerge   _____

8. concept   _____

APPLY Circle the word with the correct spelling to complete each sentence. Then write the word on the line.

9. A job that is done correctly is completed with _____.

   acurasy   accrace   accuracy   ackuerase

10. Mom placed a _____ on my scraped knee.

    bandage   baindaje   brandij   banddege

11. We need to take our car to the repair shop to have the _____ examined.

    injin   engenn   injene   engine

12. I am trying to _____ my friends to play this new board game.

    cunvinc   convince   konvense   convenje

13. A _____ is a type of government.

    democracy   dimocrassy   demockracie   damaucrusy

14. We must stick to a _____ when shopping for our family's groceries.

    budgit   budjett   budget   buddjet

Shades of Meaning

FOCUS Synonyms are words with the same or nearly the same meanings. Words with differing **shades of meaning** are similar to synonyms. Even though words with differing shades of meaning mean nearly the same thing, they have slight differences in their meanings.

Example: *small* → *tiny* → *miniscule*

At first glance, these words all have similar meanings. They all mean "little." However, as you read the words from left to right, you will notice that each of the words has a stronger level of "smallness." For example, *tiny* means lesser in size than *small*, and *miniscule* means even lesser in size than *tiny*.

PRACTICE Read each set of words. Rank the words according to their shades of meaning. The weakest or least powerful word should come first. The second weakest word should come second. The strongest or most powerful word should come third. Write the words in their correct order on the line below each set of words.

1. overjoyed, content, happy

   _____

2. hot, scorching, warm

   _____

3. clever, brilliant, intelligent

   _____

APPLY Read each pair of words. Think about the relationship between the first word and the second word. Then look at the words listed below. Write the word that has the strongest or most powerful shade of meaning on the line.

4. cool → cold → _____

   uncomfortable   freezing   weather

5. sad → depressed → _____

   terrifying   heartbroken   exhausted

6. nibble → eat → _____

   gobble   chew   picky

7. look → stare → _____

   avoid   different   glare

8. unusual → strange → _____

   bizarre   normal   reaction

9. slim → thin → _____

   allow   skinny   selfish

10. upset → angry → _____

   problem   uninterested   furious

Word Analysis • *Skills Practice*

Fluency Checklist

As you read the following passage, be sure to keep these things in mind to help you read with the appropriate rate, accuracy, and expression.

As you read, make sure you

☐ pause longer at a period or other ending punctuation.

☐ raise your voice at a question mark.

☐ use expression when you come to an exclamation point.

☐ pause at commas but not as long as you would at a period.

☐ think of the character and how he or she might say his or her words whenever you come to quotation marks.

☐ remember not to read so fast that someone listening could not hear the individual words or make sense of what is being read.

☐ stop and reread something that does not make sense.

Respecting the Land

Native Americans have always respected the land. Some tribes live on the plains. Some live in deserts. Others live in the Arctic. Each tribe has developed ways to work with the land.

The Cheyenne followed herds of bison. Their customs and way of life grew from the bison. They used bison hides wrapped around frames of wood to make teepees. The teepees were waterproof homes. They were easy to move. They could be packed up in minutes when the bison moved on.

The Navajo live in the Southwest. The land is hot and dry, with miles of dirt and clay. Long ago, the soles of their moccasins had to be sturdy. The moccasins had to protect their feet from cactus plants on the ground.

The Navajo learned many of their customs from other tribes. They learned farming and weaving from the Pueblo. They farmed corn, beans, and squash. They picked nuts and cactus fruits. They hunted prairie dogs, birds, and deer. They used deer hide to make clothing.

The Inuit live in the Artic. They have learned how to survive in their icy land. Early Inuit developed ways to stay sheltered from fierce winds. They built igloos out of blocks of snow. The Inuit hunted on land and sea. They fished. They used every part of the animal. Hides and furs were sewn into boots and warm clothing.

Life has changed for Native Americans. But all the tribes still try to keep their customs alive and still respect the land.

Spellings for the /ā/ and /əl/ Sounds

FOCUS
- /ā/ can be spelled *ai_* and *_ay*.
  Examples: *procl<u>ai</u>m, dec<u>ay</u>*
- /əl/ can be spelled *_le, _el, _al,* and *_il*.
The symbol /ə/ represents the **schwa** sound. A schwa is a vowel sound in an unstressed syllable. This means that the vowel does not take on its ordinary sound. Instead, it makes the sound you hear in the first and last letters of *America*.
Examples: *cudd<u>le</u>, cam<u>el</u>, hospit<u>al</u>,* and *penc<u>il</u>*

PRACTICE Read each word below. Circle any letters that have an /ā/ or /əl/ sound and spelling as shown in the Focus box. Cross out the word if it does not have one of these sounds and spellings.

1. embrace

2. tunnel

3. tailor

4. pair

5. capital

6. arguing

7. startle

8. yesterday

APPLY **Read each pair of words below. Circle the correct spelling.**

9. central   centril

10. dismai   dismay

11. example   exampel

12. awayt   await

Choose a word from the box to complete each sentence.

model	gerbil	mermaid	vehicle
mayor	local	tonsils	remain

13. My pet _____ escaped from his cage.

14. The town's _____ held a press conference.

15. Eliza's favorite type of _____ is a pickup truck.

16. The book's main character is a _____ who lives under the sea.

17. Next week, I will have surgery to remove my _____.

18. At the _____ farmers' market, people can buy fresh vegetables.

19. We are moving soon, so I can no longer _____ at my school.

20. You should always _____ good behavior for your siblings.

Regular Plurals

FOCUS To make many words plural, meaning "more than one," add the ending -s or -es. These types of plurals are called **regular plurals**, because they follow these rules.

- In most cases, if a word ends in a *consonant* or a *consonant* + *e*, just add -s.
  parro<u>t</u> + <u>s</u> = parro<u>ts</u>
  hou<u>se</u> + <u>s</u> = hou<u>ses</u>

- The letters -es are added to words ending in *ch, sh, s, ss, ff, x, z,* or *zz*.
  bo<u>x</u> + <u>es</u> = bo<u>xes</u>

- If a word ends in a *consonant* + *y*, change the *y* to *i*, and add -es.
  lad<u>y</u> + <u>es</u> = lad<u>ies</u>

- If a word ends in *f* or *fe*, change the *f* or *fe* to *v*, and add -es.
  kni<u>fe</u> + <u>es</u> = kni<u>ves</u>

PRACTICE Circle the correct spelling for each word. Write the correct spelling on the line.

1. pillow: pillowes   pillows   _____
2. berry: berrys   berries   _____
3. cowboy: cowboys   cowboies   _____
4. loaf: loafs   loaves   _____
5. porch: porches   porchies   _____
6. suitcase: suitcasees   suitcases   _____

APPLY Think about how to make each word from the box plural. Sort the plural words into the correct groups and write the words on the lines below.

life	satellite	mystery	hoof	slide
problem	beach	donkey	diary	rosebush

Group 1: Add -s

7. _____

8. _____

9. _____

10. _____

Group 2: Add -es

11. _____

12. _____

Group 3: Change y to i and add -es

13. _____

14. _____

Group 4: Change f or fe to v and add -es

15. _____

16. _____

Fluency Checklist

As you read the following passage, be sure to keep these things in mind to help you read with the appropriate rate, accuracy, and expression.

As you read, make sure you

☐ pause longer at a period or other ending punctuation.

☐ raise your voice at a question mark.

☐ use expression when you come to an exclamation point.

☐ pause at commas but not as long as you would at a period.

☐ think of the character and how he or she might say his or her words whenever you come to quotation marks.

☐ remember not to read so fast that someone listening could not hear the individual words or make sense of what is being read.

☐ stop and reread something that does not make sense.

Saving the Falcons

High above the Brooklyn Bridge, a peregrine falcon circles. On the bridge is a wildlife biologist named Chris. The falcon watches him closely. He looks at three baby falcons in their nest. It is eighty feet above the traffic!

Chris will not harm this falcon family. He's one of many people helping falcons. These people respect falcons and the role they play in nature. Falcons were once an endangered species. Now they are making a comeback. Chris will place bands around the young birds' legs. The band will aid in tracking them. Then Chris will put the baby birds safely back in the nest.

Peregrine falcons were once common in mountain areas. Then they almost disappeared. People hunted them. People stole their eggs. Chemicals nearly wiped them out. Today, falcons live in the wild again. Some live in New York City and other big cities. How did this happen?

The peregrine falcon was on its way to extinction. Concerned people began raising falcons. They hoped they could rescue the birds. They did not release them into the wild though. Predators lived there and the young falcons would be in danger. They decided to release them in cities instead.

There, people like Chris began looking after the falcons. They do this because they respect the natural world. They feel that animals should be treated kindly. Humans almost destroyed the falcons. Now humans are helping bring them back.

So next time you are in a big city, look up. You may see a falcon on the hunt. And you can feel happy that peregrine falcons are alive and well. Thanks to caring people, they will not disappear from our world.

Fluency • *Skills Practice*

Spellings for the /f/, /m/, /n/, /r/, and /w/ Sounds

FOCUS
- /**f**/ can be spelled *ph*.
  Examples: *ph*ase, orp*h*an
- /**m**/ can be spelled *_mb*.
  Examples: cli*mb*, nu*mb*
- /**n**/ can be spelled *kn_*.
  Examples: *kn*itting, *kn*oll
- /**r**/ can be spelled *wr_*.
  Examples: *wr*ongful, *wr*estler
- /**w**/ can be spelled *wh_*.
  Examples: *wh*istle, *wh*iteboard

PRACTICE Sort the words below. Write each word under the correct heading.

bomb	knotted	wristband	biographer	knack
photo	wheezing	comb	wheelchair	wraparound

/f/ = ph   **/m/ = _mb**   **/n/ = kn_**

1. _____   3. _____   5. _____

2. _____   4. _____   6. _____

/r/ = wr_   **/w/ = wh_**

7. _____   9. _____

8. _____   10. _____

APPLY Read each sentence. Choose the correct spelling
of the word underneath that completes the sentence. Write
the word on the blank line.

11. Calling someone _____ is a very mean thing to do.
    (dumb, dumm)

12. A _____ is a section of written text in a book.
    (paragraf, paragraph)

13. I wear a _____ when I am away from home.
    (ristwatch, wristwatch)

14. Kyle has to _____ down to give his little brother a hug.
    (kneel, neel)

15. Bridget uses special toothpaste to keep her teeth
    _____.
    (wite, white)

16. We were punished for a _____.
    (wrongdoing, rongdoing)

17. Our teacher taught us a new _____ lesson.
    (phonics, fonics)

18. Investigators examined the _____ left behind by
    the thief.
    (thumprint, thumbprint)

Irregular Plurals

FOCUS **Irregular plurals** do not follow the regular pattern.

- Some words, such as *deer* and *shrimp*, have the same singular and plural forms.

- Some words, such as *goose*, change spellings in the plural form. In the plural form, *goose* becomes *geese*.
  Examples: *cri<u>sis</u>, cri<u>ses</u>*   *cact<u>us</u>, cact<u>i</u>*

PRACTICE Sort each word from the box under the correct heading below.

children	teeth	fish
sheep	mice	women

Words with the same singular and plural

1. _____

2. _____

Words with spelling changes

3. _____

4. _____

5. _____

6. _____

APPLY Read each singular noun. Circle the correct irregular plural form of the noun. (Remember: Some words have the same singular and plural forms.)

7. person: persons   **people**

8. tuna: tuna   tunas

9. bacterium: bacteria   bacteriums

10. species: specieses   species

11. elk: elk   elks

12. nucleus: nucleuses   nuclei

13. salmon: salmons   salmon

14. headquarters: headquarters   headquarter

15. ox: oxens   oxen

16. trout: trout   trouts

Word Analysis • *Skills Practice*

Fluency Checklist

As you read the following passage, be sure to keep these things in mind to help you read with the appropriate rate, accuracy, and expression.

As you read, make sure you

☐   pause longer at a period or other ending punctuation.

☐   raise your voice at a question mark.

☐   use expression when you come to an exclamation point.

☐   pause at commas but not as long as you would at a period.

☐   think of the character and how he or she might say his or her words whenever you come to quotation marks.

☐   remember not to read so fast that someone listening could not hear the individual words or make sense of what is being read.

☐   stop and reread something that does not make sense.

For Love of the Game!

My name is Katy, and my best friend is Mia. We love to play soccer! Mia is always giving me support, and I give it right back.

We play on the same team, the Stingers. I am the goalie but Mia is our best player. Her upbeat attitude inspires everyone on the team. She makes everyone else a better player.

When the season began, everything seemed to go wrong. Mia reminded us that having fun was the object of the game. She helped us focus on having fun. Soon we were improving and Mia was the secret to our success. With her skill and positive attitude, we started winning!

By our final game, we were playing great! Some of the girls started thinking we could not be beat. The game was a close battle; neither side could get a goal. Then in the final minute of the first half, the other team scored.

At halftime, someone said it was my fault. Others agreed. Mia spoke up. "We got this far by playing as a team. It isn't Katy's fault they scored. It is the team's fault. They kicked a good shot. They played better than us. We don't try to blame one person; we are a team. We win or lose as a team. That is how you show respect to your teammates. And your friends."

I was so happy we were friends! The other girls looked a little ashamed. They agreed that Mia was right. If we hadn't played as a team, we never would have made it this far. We agreed to have fun during the second half. We were going to finish this game as a team. And it really didn't matter who won; we were winners already!

Fluency • *Skills Practice*

Fluency Checklist

As you read the following passage, be sure to keep these things in mind to help you read with the appropriate rate, accuracy, and expression.

As you read, make sure you

☐ pause longer at a period or other ending punctuation.

☐ raise your voice at a question mark.

☐ use expression when you come to an exclamation point.

☐ pause at commas but not as long as you would at a period.

☐ think of the character and how he or she might say his or her words whenever you come to quotation marks.

☐ remember not to read so fast that someone listening could not hear the individual words or make sense of what is being read.

☐ stop and reread something that does not make sense.

Friends around the World

Do you have a good friend? What makes you good friends? Do you play with your friend? Do you talk on the phone? Do you share secrets? Would you do a favor for your friend?

You probably know that friends are important. You probably do not know that Congress has set aside a day for friends. It is the first Sunday in August.

Friendship Day in the United States began in 1937. Some other countries followed our tradition with their own day for friends, including India. Best friends like to spend Friendship Day together in India.

Friendship Day is also important in parts of South America. It is held on July 20. People go to parties to meet new friends on this day.

The Irish have a special ring to wear for friendship. On it, there is a crown resting on top of a heart, being held by two hands. Each part has a meaning. The crown stands for loyalty, the heart stands for love, and the hands stand for friendship.

Some friends eat a meal together on Friendship Day. Some people send cards to their friends. There are many ways to show your friends how you feel about them!

In 1997, the United Nations started a plan for having a Friendship Day too. Friendships can heal bad feelings that people have about each other. It would be great if friendship could bring all people together.

Think about your friends. How do you honor friendship? What do you share with your friends? How does friendship bring you together with other people?

Fluency • *Skills Practice*

Name _____ Date _____

Fluency Checklist

As you read the following passage, be sure to keep these things in mind to help you read with the appropriate rate, accuracy, and expression.

As you read, make sure you

☐ pause longer at a period or other ending punctuation.

☐ raise your voice at a question mark.

☐ use expression when you come to an exclamation point.

☐ pause at commas but not as long as you would at a period.

☐ think of the character and how he or she might say his or her words whenever you come to quotation marks.

☐ remember not to read so fast that someone listening could not hear the individual words or make sense of what is being read.

☐ stop and reread something that does not make sense.

Horse and Dog

One day, a farmer loaded his horse, got his dog, and set off to the market. Halfway there, the farmer decided to take a nap.

Horse began to chomp eagerly on the grass. Dog was also hungry. She looked hopefully at one of the sacks on Horse's back.

"Do me a favor, friend," Dog said to Horse. "My food is in a small bag on your back and I am too small to jump up and reach it. Please pull it down for me."

"I don't want to, Dog. I am busy eating right now. Wait for the man to wake up," Horse replied. "He will get your food for you as he always does."

Dog knew the man would be angry if she woke him up. She looked at Horse and shook her head sadly. Then she sighed and settled down to wait.

A hungry wolf sneaked out of the woods and spotted Horse. She smiled and thought, *That little horse would make a wonderful meal.*

Horse spotted the wolf heading straight toward him. "Do me a favor, friend!" Horse whispered to Dog. "Help me fight Wolf. We can work together to chase her away!"

Dog did not move. "I don't want to, Horse. I am busy resting right now. Wait for the man to wake up," she replied. "He will save you as he always does."

Poor Horse ran off and the hungry wolf followed him. Finally, Dog came to Horse's aid. They chased off the wolf. By then, Horse had learned his lesson. *To* have *good friends, you must* be *a good friend,* he thought as he helped Dog with her food.

Spellings for the /ē/ Sound

FOCUS
- /ē/ can be spelled ee.
  Examples: *fr<u>ee</u>zer, chimpanz<u>ee</u>*
- /ē/ can be spelled ea.
  Examples: *b<u>ea</u>gle, f<u>ea</u>ture*
- /ē/ can be spelled _y.
  Examples: *glor<u>y</u>, temporar<u>y</u>*
- /ē/ can be spelled ie_.
  Examples: *y<u>ie</u>ld, retr<u>ie</u>ve*
- /ē/ can be spelled _ey.
  Examples: *journ<u>ey</u>, attorn<u>ey</u>*

PRACTICE Read each word. Circle the long /ē/ spelling in each word.

1. freedom

2. battery

3. cashier

4. eastern

5. fantasy

6. beetle

7. monkey

8. university

APPLY Read each set of words below. Circle the correct spelling.

9.   acheeve   achieve   acheyve

10.   grumpy   grumpie   grumpey

11.   disiese   diseese   disease

12.   mony   money   monie

Read the rough draft of the paragraph below. Cross out the six spelling errors. Write the correct spellings above the crossed-out words.

A Rough Day on the Baseball Field

My baseball team had a tough game today. Our goal in every game is

to succead. However, it is not always possible to win every game. Today

we lost to a very good team—the Huskies. We were defieted by a score

of 4–3. Late into the game, the score was tied. Evan, our star outfeelder,

caught a fly ball. It was a perfect catch. Unfortunately, his jersy got

twisted around. His arm almost came out of his shirt sleeve! This caused

him to become distracted, and he fell to the ground. After Evan landed on

the ground, he tried to keep the baseball in his glove. Finalley, he gained

control of the situation. He made the catch after all! However, on the very

next play, the Huskies scored a run. They won the game, but we were all

proud of Evan for his amazing recoverey of the ball.

Contractions and Possessives

FOCUS
- A **contraction** is formed from combining two words. Some letters are left out when the words combine. An apostrophe (') marks the spot where the letters were dropped.

    Example: *they + have = they've*

    Some contractions look the same but have different meanings. For example, *he'd* can mean "he had" or "he would."

- A **possessive noun** shows who or what owns or possesses something. Consider the following question: "Whose blanket is this?" Answer: "This blanket belongs to Shelley. It is *Shelley's* blanket." *Shelley's* is the possessive noun.

    If a word is a *singular noun*, add an apostrophe + -s: ('s).   Example: *alligator's*

    If a word is a *regular plural noun*, add an apostrophe after the -s: (s').   Example: *alligators'*

    If a word is an *irregular plural noun* that does not end in -s, add 's.   Example: *children's*

PRACTICE Write the words that combine to make each contraction. Some contractions can be made by two sets of words.

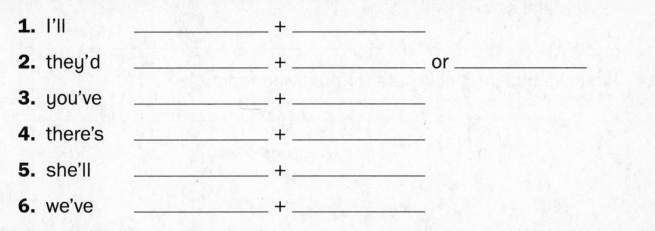

1. I'll   _____ + _____

2. they'd   _____ + _____ or _____

3. you've   _____ + _____

4. there's   _____ + _____

5. she'll   _____ + _____

6. we've   _____ + _____

APPLY **Read the first sentence. Then read the second sentence. Write the possessive form of the underlined word on the line.**

7. The skin of the <u>alligator</u> is beginning to peel.

The _____ skin is beginning to peel.

8. A local group of <u>churches</u> operates a daycare center; it is popular with many parents.

The _____ daycare center is popular with many parents.

9. The wings of the <u>butterfly</u> are a bright orange and blue color.

The _____ wings are a bright orange and blue color.

10. A center for <u>women</u> provides many healthcare services.

The _____ center provides many healthcare services.

Read each sentence below. Circle the pair of words that can be made into contractions. Write each contraction on the line below.

11. Sasha would have gone to the fair, but she needed to do her chores.

_____

12. Mark wants to go to college, so he is studying very hard in order to get good grades.

_____

13. My sisters are both teachers and they are helping each other create lesson plans.

_____

14. We have bought a new sofa for our living room.

_____

Word Analysis • *Skills Practice*

In the Desert (part 1)

Miguel and his family were visiting his grandfather in Arizona. It was spring, and Miguel was interested in one thing: baseball. Spring training was in progress and Miguel wanted to be a part of it. But his family had other ideas. They wanted to visit the desert and see the diverse plant and animal life. That morning, they set off on a hike. Grandpa was going to show them around the ecosystem he admired so much.

As his family was sitting and resting, Miguel was bored. He inspected the flat desert landscape around him. *Why are we hiking around out here?* he thought. He paid little attention to Grandpa's explanation about the desert ecosystem around them. But his sister Carmen was listening intently to every word.

"If we could see inside these holes, or burrows, we would see animals resting," Grandpa said. As he spoke, he pointed to little holes near the side of the trail. For the first time all day, Miguel became interested. Looking around the barren desert, he never would have thought he was surrounded by animals.

"How can animals live in such a hot, dry place?" Miguel asked. Grandpa smiled. He realized Miguel had barely paid attention earlier.

Before Grandpa could respond, Carmen said, "They stay underground, where it is cool. Their burrows protect them from the hot sun. They don't come out until evening, when the sun has gone down. It's not nearly so hot then."

Grandpa's smile widened because he knew Carmen had been paying attention. "That's right," declared Grandpa. He went on, "I can't identify the animal just by looking at the hole, but a kangaroo rat may live in that one."

"Rats as big as kangaroos!" Miguel exclaimed.

Grandpa chuckled and said, "Kangaroo rats are small and look like mice. They rest during the day. But at night they venture out to collect seeds."

Too bad; this was just about to get interesting, Miguel thought.

Spellings for the /ī/ Sound

FOCUS
- /ī/ can be spelled _igh.
  Examples: *ton<u>igh</u>t, ins<u>igh</u>t*
- /ī/ can be spelled _ie.
  Examples: *def<u>ie</u>d, simplif<u>ie</u>d*
- /ī/ can be spelled _y.
  Examples: *den<u>y</u>, unif<u>y</u>*

PRACTICE Read each word below. Write *Long i* if the word has one of the /ī/ spellings as shown in the Focus box above. Write *No* if it does not.

1. instant _____

2. frighten _____

3. happy _____

4. died _____

5. hyper _____

6. prairies _____

7. daylight _____

8. eight _____

9. simply _____

10. hairstyle _____

APPLY Write a word from the box to complete each sentence. Next to the word, write the /ī/ spelling that the word contains: _igh, _ie, or _y.

butterflies	horrify	midnight	skyscrapers
supplied	nightmare	lightning	satisfied

11. The ending of my favorite scary book tends to

_____ me every time I read it.

12. I was _____ with the grade I received on my

English paper.

13. Aimee, my little sister, was very scared after she had a

_____ last night.

14. Our teacher _____ us with markers and

drawing paper.

15. When the clock strikes _____, a new day

begins.

16. New York City has many tall _____.

17. We visited a nature museum and saw many colorful

_____.

18. The _____ struck, followed by the sound

of a thundering boom.

Irregular Verbs and Abstract Nouns

FOCUS
- **Irregular verbs** are verbs that do not follow a normal pattern. With **regular verbs**, the inflectional ending *-ed* is added to the present tense of a verb to make it past tense.
  Examples: *walk* (present), *walked* (past)
  dance (present), *danced* (past)
  Irregular verbs take on different forms in the past tense. They do not include the *-ed* ending.
  Examples: *hold* (present), *held* (past)
  build (present), *built* (past)

- **Abstract nouns** are words that you are unable to experience with your five senses. You cannot see, hear, smell, taste, or touch them. For example, *cat* and *sandwich* are not abstract nouns, because you can observe them with your senses. Instead, abstract nouns are ideas or concepts. These words make you feel or think about something. For example, *greed* and *peace* are abstract nouns.

PRACTICE Read each word below. Each word is a present-tense irregular verb. Then circle the correct past-tense form of that verb from the pair of words provided.

1. meet: meeted   met

2. fight: fighted   fought

3. tell: told   telled

Read the sets of words below. Circle the abstract noun in each set of words.

4. rainbow   honesty   grandmother

5. importance   parrot   banana

6. lightning   computer   anger

APPLY Read each sentence below. Look at the underlined word in each sentence. Write the correct past tense of each irregular verb on the line.

7. Dante <u>find</u> the missing book underneath his bed.

_____

8. The students <u>understand</u> that they had one hour to complete

the test. _____

9. After I visited my sick friend, I <u>feel</u> a fever and sore throat begin

to come on. _____

Read each sentence below. Choose the correct abstract noun to complete each sentence. Write the word on the line.

friendship	knowledge	fantasy

10. The plot of the movie was based on _____, rather than reality.

11. I respect and value my _____ with Kane.

12. Colin's _____ of historical events amazed his Social Studies teacher.

Wild Wetlands

Did you know that all the living things in an ecosystem depend on each other? These connections are called interdependence. They help all living things in the ecosystem meet their needs to survive.

Take wetlands for example. If the tiny swamp creatures vanish, the mighty alligator might not survive either. What if certain plants no longer can grow? The animals in the ecosystem will suffer too. That is because they are all part of a food chain.

A food chain shows where living things receive their energy. At the beginning of the food chain are plants. Plants make their own food. Because they make food, they are called the *producers* in the food chain. Wetland producers range from marsh grass to huge cypress trees.

Wetland animals get their energy by eating plants and other animals. They are the *consumers* in the food chain. What animals eat determines their place in the chain.

Some consumers, called herbivores, eat nothing but plants. Rabbits and squirrels are herbivores.

Other consumers, called carnivores, eat only other animals. Alligators and bobcats are two kinds of wetland carnivores.

Some consumers eat both plants and animals. These animals are omnivores. Black bears are an omnivore.

All plants and animals eventually die. When they do, they are "eaten" by decomposers. Bacteria are decomposers that are found everywhere. But because they are so tiny, you won't be able to see them without a microscope.

Fungi are another small decomposer. Both are very powerful. They can digest even the largest plants and animals over time. The remains enter the soil and water as nutrients. These nutrients help plants grow. This leads back to the beginning of the food chain.

When you look at a food chain, it shows a balance in an ecosystem. This balance is what allows an ecosystem to survive.

Spellings for the /ō/ Sound

FOCUS • /ō/ can be spelled oa_.
Examples: m<u>oa</u>n, sailb<u>oa</u>t
• /ō/ can be spelled _ow.
Examples: bell<u>ow</u>, rainb<u>ow</u>

PRACTICE Read each sentence below. Choose the word with the correct /ō/ spelling as shown in the Focus box above to complete each sentence. Write the word on the blank line.

1. Mom toasted the _____ over the campfire.
(marshmalloa, marshmallow)

2. A hurricane was moving over the southern
_____ areas.
(cowstal, coastal)

3. The bright _____ sun rose in the sky.
(yellow, yelloa)

4. I tried to _____ the rabbit to come out
of its cage. (coax, cowx)

5. A _____ is a kind of tree; its wood is used
(willoa, willow)
to make several products.

6. The uneven _____ tracks made for a bumpy ride.
(railrowd, railroad)

APPLY Select the word from the word box that matches the clue or definition below. Write the word on the line.

burrow	wheelbarrow	hoax	groaning
oatmeal	sorrow	goal	mellow

7. A small cart with one wheel that is used for yard work.

_____

8. A breakfast food that is made of ground-up grains.

_____

9. A sound someone makes when in pain or misery.

_____

10. Having a calm, relaxed manner.

_____

11. To make a tunnel by digging into the ground, as an animal might do.

_____

12. Something that a person wishes to accomplish or achieve.

_____

13. Extreme sadness or grief.

_____

14. An act intended to trick or deceive.

_____

Homophones

> **FOCUS** **Homophones** are words that sound alike but have different spellings and different meanings. Think about the meaning of the word when deciding how to spell a homophone correctly.
>
> Example: *sea* and *see* are homophones.
>
> The words sound like: *sea* (sē)   *see* (sē)
>
> But they have different meanings:
>
> *sea* "a large body of saltwater"
>
> *see* "to look at with the eyes"

PRACTICE **Read the sentences. Then answer the questions below.**

Katie <u>heard</u> a loud noise in the distance. She later discovered the sound was caused by a <u>herd</u> of elephants.

1. What is the meaning of *heard* in the first sentence?

_____

2. What is the meaning of *herd* in the second sentence?

_____

3. The words *heard* and *herd* are homophones. What do the two words have in common? _____

4. Use *heard* or *herd* to complete the following sentence:
In the 1800s, it was common for people to see a
_____ of buffalo.

APPLY Read each pair of sentences, and identify which words sound alike. Circle the homophones in the sentences. On the lines below, provide a definition for each homophone.

5. My dad stepped on the car's brake to come to a stop.

   I took a break from doing my homework.

   _____

   _____

6. They must wait twenty minutes before the soccer game begins.

   The weight of the box is fifty pounds.

   _____

   _____

7. Many bridges and large buildings are made of steel.

   The thief attempted to steal from a store, but he was caught.

   _____

   _____

8. Josh watched a dog nervously bury his bone in the ground.

   My favorite type of berry is the blueberry.

   _____

   _____

Word Analysis • *Skills Practice*

In the Desert (part 2)

Grandpa continued to explain how kangaroo rats survived in the desert. Miguel might have been bored, but Carmen was not. Carmen was listening with great interest. "How do kangaroo rats get their water? Can they get it from seeds?" she asked.

Miguel couldn't believe Carmen asked that. *Who ever heard of animals getting water from seeds?* he thought. *At least she doesn't know everything.*

But before Miguel could respond, Grandpa answered. "Yes, Carmen, kangaroo rats are extraordinary animals. They have adapted to their environment. They can get water even from dry seeds. Then they store them in their burrows."

Miguel was stunned. Carmen looked proud. *Maybe she does know everything,* Miguel thought. The idea of that worried him. To change the subject, he quickly asked another question.

"If they're so small, why are they called kangaroo rats?"

As he asked, Miguel gazed out at the desert, hoping to see a kangaroo rat. Baseball was no longer the only thing he wanted to think about. *Who knew the desert was so full of life?* he thought. He was quickly becoming as interested as Carmen.

"Well, they have large hind legs that let them leap rapidly from predators," explained Grandpa. "At night, the desert comes alive. Animals come out looking for food. Some animals, like kangaroo rats, look for seeds and plants. They have adapted to eat what the desert makes available. Other animals in the food chain, like snakes and owls, are predators. They like to make a dinner out of smaller animals."

"Wow, it's a jungle out there!" exclaimed Miguel. Carmen groaned at his terrible sense of humor. "No, a jungle is a *completely* different ecosystem," she responded. The whole family joined in the laughter, and Miguel vowed to pay more attention. *Who would have thought there was so much life in the desert?* he thought as they moved on.

Spellings for the /ū/ Sound

FOCUS
- /ū/ can be spelled _ew.
  Examples: *few*, *yew*
- /ū/ can be spelled _ue.
  Examples: *discontinued*, *argues*

PRACTICE Read each word below. Circle any letters that have one of the /ū/ spellings as shown in the Focus box above. Cross out the word if it does not have the /ū/ sound spelled _ew or _ue.

1. curfew

2. cute

3. barbecues

4. brunch

5. chew

6. cupid

7. miscue

8. support

9. fewer

10. juice

APPLY Write a word from the box to complete each sentence. Below the sentence, circle the /ū/ spelling the word contains.

value	rescuers	continue
pews	argued	fewer

11. The church _____ were made of a dark wood.

The word has the /ū/ sound spelled: _ew, _ue

12. The sisters _____ over who won the board game.

The word has the /ū/ sound spelled: _ew, _ue

13. The _____ of this baseball card is four dollars.

The word has the /ū/ sound spelled: _ew, _ue

14. I'm excited to _____ reading my book.

The word has the /ū/ sound spelled: _ew, _ue

15. The _____ helped the people stranded on the boat.

The word has the /ū/ sound spelled: _ew, _ue

16. Marissa has _____ than twenty dollars left in her bank account.

The word has the /ū/ sound spelled: _ew, _ue

Homographs and Multiple-Meaning Words

> **FOCUS** **Homographs** and **multiple-meaning words** are words that share the same spellings but have different meanings. They may or may not have different pronunciations. Homographs also have different origins. Use a dictionary to determine if a word is a homograph or a multiple-meaning word.
>
> Homograph example: *desert*
>
> The words sound like: *desert* (dez' ərt)   *desert* (di' zərt)
>
> They have different meanings: *desert* "a hot, sandy area"   *desert* "to abandon"
>
> And they have different origins: Middle English   Latin
>
> Multiple-Meaning Word example: *nail*
>
> The words sound like: *nail* (nāl)   *nail* (nāl)
>
> But they have different meanings: *nail* "a piece of metal"   *nail* "covering of a finger or toe"

PRACTICE Read each pair of sentences. Then read the definitions for the missing words. Fill in the blanks with the correct homograph or multiple-meaning word.

1. Dave _____ the room when it became too noisy.

   Definition 1: "went away"

   Should Kristin turn right or _____ at the stop sign?

   Definition 2: "a specific direction"

2. I burnt my hand and now I have a fresh _____.

Definition 1: "an injury"

Katie _____ up the rope before putting it away.

Definition 2: "wrapped into a coil"

APPLY Choose the word whose meanings fit both sentences. Circle the correct word. Then write the word on each line to complete the sentences.

3. Adrian has to _____ his clothes before playing outside.

Jenna found some extra _____ in her purse.

> **brick**   **worry**   **change**   **blue**

4. The musician played the _____ guitar in his band.

I caught a _____ while fishing with my dad.

> **house**   **bass**   **lonely**   **different**

5. The deer ran across the treeless, open _____.

I wore a very _____ and simple outfit.

> **area**   **bossy**   **water**   **plain**

6. The director of the play will _____ our performance.

Do you have a written _____ of this meeting?

> **record**   **shape**   **present**   **treasure**

7. We need to _____ the box shut.

Henry took a picture of a _____ resting on an iceberg.

> **seal**   **pigeon**   **mile**   **tuck**

8. The class has one _____ to complete this brief activity.

My problem is _____ compared to your much larger one.

> **dusk**   **gesture**   **minute**   **hour**

Word Analysis • *Skills Practice*

Animal Builders

Many animals construct their own homes. These homes protect them from predators and bad weather. In these homes they store food and raise their young. Some examples include honeybees, beavers, termites, and many birds.

Another notable example is the prairie dog. Let's examine how prairie dogs group together to construct homes. These homes help them survive.

Prairie dogs are small rodents. They belong to the squirrel family. They weigh from one to three pounds. They are twelve to sixteen inches tall. One of their main habitats is the Great Plains of the United States.

Prairie dogs create their homes, or "towns," by carving out tunnels under the ground. The entrances can be found easily enough. There is always a large pile of dirt around each tunnel opening.

To construct the tunnels, prairie dogs dig downward several feet. Then they level off the tunnels and extend them up to fifty feet. They make side tunnels that are used as escape routes in case of danger. The tunnels let fresh air blow through the different rooms in the town.

Towns can vary in size. The can cover an area from one acre to one thousand acres. There may be up to thirty-five prairie dogs in one acre. In the early 1900s an enormous prairie dog town was discovered in Texas. It was 250 miles long and 100 miles wide!

Prairie dogs are social animals. They live in *coteries*, or families. Prairie dog coteries take part in group activities. They visit with and groom each other. They eat together and they work together. They help each other watch for danger. They show how one form of group behavior can help animals survive.

Prairie dogs are just one example of how group behavior can help animals survive. But there are many more examples that are worth learning about on your own.

Spellings for the /o͞o/ Sound

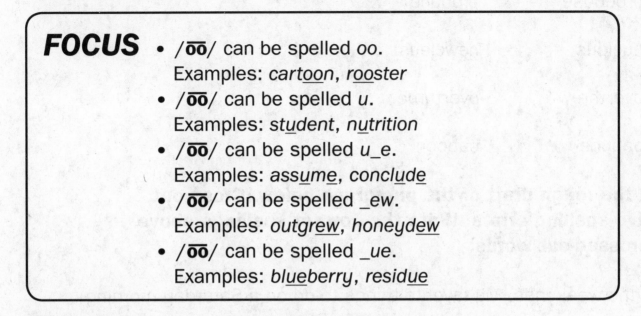

FOCUS
- /o͞o/ can be spelled oo.
  Examples: *cart__oo__n, r__oo__ster*
- /o͞o/ can be spelled u.
  Examples: *st__u__dent, n__u__trition*
- /o͞o/ can be spelled u_e.
  Examples: *ass__u__me, concl__u__de*
- /o͞o/ can be spelled _ew.
  Examples: *outgr__ew__, honeyd__ew__*
- /o͞o/ can be spelled _ue.
  Examples: *bl__ue__berry, resid__ue__*

PRACTICE Write the words from the word box in alphabetical order. Circle the letters that spell the /o͞o/ sound.

fluid	mildew	costume
lagoon	untrue	jewelry

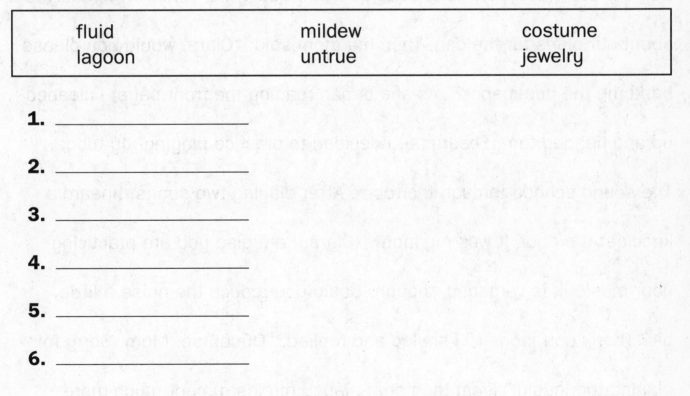

1. _____

2. _____

3. _____

4. _____

5. _____

6. _____

APPLY Read each pair of words. Circle the word with the correct /o͞o/ spelling.

7. prodoose   produce

8. nucleus   newcleus

9. overthrew   overthrue

10. babune   baboon

Read the rough draft of the paragraph below. Cross out the five spelling errors. Write the correct spellings above the crossed-out words.

I love the weekends. My favorite things to do on a Saturday morning

are to relax and pursoo my hobbies. This morning, my mother and I sat

down to eat breakfast. As the sun peered through the window, we chatted

about our plans for the day. Then my mom said, "Clara, would you please

hand me the nuespaper?" As she began reading the front page, I cleaned

up and headed to my bedrume. I decided to practice playing my tubea.

The sound echoed through the room. After playing two songs, I heard a

knock at the door. It was my mom. "Clara, I am glad you are practicing

your music. It is very loud, though. Could you reduce the noise a little

bit? Thank you, honey." I smiled and replied, "Of course, Mom. Sorry for

playing tue loudly." From then on, I played my instrument much more

quietly.

Homographs and Multiple-Meaning Words

> **FOCUS** **Homographs** and **multiple-meaning words** are words that share the same spellings but have different meanings. They may or may not have different pronunciations. Homographs also have different origins. Use a dictionary to determine if a word is a homograph or a multiple-meaning word.
>
> | Homograph | Multiple-Meaning Word |
> |---|---|
> | *pound* | *subject* |
> | *pownd/pownd* | *səb' jekt/səb jekt'* |
>
> 1. "a unit of weight" (from Latin)
>
> 2. "to strike something" (from Old English)
>
> 1. "a specialized area of knowledge"
>
> 2. "expose to something unwanted"

PRACTICE **Read the two sentences. Circle the homographs in the sentences.**

Sentence 1: The leaves begin to grow on trees in the spring.

Sentence 2: The baby laughed as she watched the cat spring into the air.

1. Read the two definitions below. Write *Sentence 1* next to the definition that correctly matches the meaning of the word used in the first sentence. Write *Sentence 2* next to the definition that correctly matches the meaning of the word used in the second sentence.

"to leap" _____

"the season between winter and summer" _____

2. Write your own sentences using the homograph *spring*. Each sentence should use a different definition of the word.

_____

_____

APPLY Read each sentence. Look at the underlined word. Then read the two definitions provided. Circle the definition that accurately matches the meaning of the word in the sentence.

3. After standing for an hour, I began to <u>lean</u> against the wall.

    a. "to place one's weight against something for support"
    b. "having little or no fat"

4. We visited the nature <u>reserve</u> on our field trip.

    a. "to make arrangements for use at a later time"
    b. "an area of land given special protection"

5. Shayna was careful not to <u>steer</u> her bicycle into the road.

    a. "to direct the course of something"
    b. "a type of male animal used as livestock"

6. My cousin has set a <u>date</u> for his wedding.

    a. "a period of time in which an expected event will occur"
    b. "a small fruit"

7. There are enough computers in the classroom for each <u>pupil</u>.

    a. "an opening located in the center of the eye"
    b. "a young person in school"

8. The band director will <u>conduct</u> his students during the concert.

    a. "to lead or direct"
    b. "the way that a person acts or behaves"

Word Analysis • *Skills Practice*

Galápagos Islands

The Galápagos Islands are home to some strange plants and animals. Located 600 miles from South America, they are isolated in the Pacific Ocean. This isolation is why the islands are so special. And the unique species that live there require the ecosystem that only those islands provide.

The plants and animals that have lived there adapted to their habitat. Each had developed its own role to keep the ecosystem healthy, until another species—humans—discovered the islands. In the 1800s, people began coming to the Galápagos Islands. Little did they know they were changing the habitat.

People hoped to farm on the islands. They brought new animals to raise. The native species had new competition for their habitat. Animals such as giant tortoises, sea turtles, and ground-nesting birds were affected. They were not used to competing with these newcomers. Animals like pigs trampled their nests and ate their eggs. Fewer native animals were born. That made the food chain unbalanced.

Humans also overfished around the Galápagos. They were catching too many sea cucumbers. At the time, they didn't realize that these animals kept the ecosystem in balance. Sea cucumbers look strange, but they perform an important role. They break down the ocean floor. That allows plants to grow down there. Without sea cucumbers, the ocean floor hardens. Plants can't take root. By wiping out the sea cucumbers, humans wiped out the habitat for many other creatures.

Giant tortoises were also affected by people. Weighing 500 pounds or more, these tortoises had no predators. That changed when humans arrived. Humans were now at the top of the food chain. The tortoises could not adapt to this change. Big and slow, the tortoises made easy prey. Before humans arrived, there were about 250,000 tortoises. Now there are less than 20,000.

Efforts are being made to save the islands. Humans have realized the damage they have done. The special ecosystem will be saved and people will be able to enjoy it for years to come.

In the Desert (part 3)

Miguel and his family moved on, continuing their hike through the desert. Baseball was the furthest thing from his mind. Now all he could think about was the hidden ecosystem around him.

Miguel looked around and inspected the desert. In the bright sun, it stretched on for miles. The family walked on. After a few minutes of silence, Miguel spoke up.

"Boy, is it hot! That sun is blazing! I guess wearing long pants wasn't a good idea."

Grandpa responded, "Actually, wearing long pants was an excellent idea. It's good protection for your legs. Remember all those holes we saw? Well, a kangaroo rat isn't the only thing that might live in those. Rattlesnakes can take over the burrows of animals that live in the ground. It's always good to have protection out here in the desert."

"Yikes, rattlesnakes?" Miguel shuddered. Snakes were one animal Miguel was not hoping to see!

"Yes, rattlesnakes," said Grandpa. "Do you recall what I told you before we began the hike? A rattlesnake bite can make you very ill. Your pants help protect your legs from snakes. They can also protect you from the sun too. As you noticed, it can get mighty hot out here. Covering up will protect your skin and keep you cool."

"Never mind the sun," Miguel said. "I want to know more about rattlesnakes. Didn't you say earlier that a rattlesnake only bites people if it's attacked or frightened?"

"That's correct," said Grandpa, "and it is more likely to run away or hide. Remember, you have to be mindful of where you're hiking. Rattlesnakes like to bask in the sun. They absorb the heat to stay warm. If you unexpectedly step right next to a rattlesnake, it might strike. That's a good reason to stay on the trails."

I'd better pay more attention to where I step, Miguel thought. But he quickly turned his attention back to Grandpa.

In the Desert (part 4)

Miguel listened intently. Grandpa was vividly describing other animals that dug holes in the desert ecosystem. Miguel was still astonished he hadn't seen the holes earlier.

As Grandpa talked, Miguel became more inquisitive. He asked Grandpa detailed and intricate questions. As a result, Miguel learned about some really fascinating animals. Colonies of bats, jackrabbits with huge ears, scorpions, coyotes, and many more. They were all hiding, possibly nearby, until the daytime ended and the sun went down. Somehow, all these animals had adapted ways to survive in the desert. Miguel was amazed. It was unbelievable that so many animals could survive in such a hot and dusty place.

The family walked a little longer. Then Grandpa announced, "Let's take a breather. We'll rest on these boulders for a few minutes. Then we'll hike back. But remember, beware of where you sit!"

Miguel knew that near and underneath rocks, strange-looking and sometimes dangerous creatures lurked. He located a safe rock to sit on. But he couldn't stop picturing rattlesnakes just behind it. And scorpions crawling underneath it. And spiders spinning webs on its sides. *Maybe I'll just stand,* Miguel thought.

Once everyone else was done resting, the family began walking again. Grandpa kept talking. And Miguel kept searching for a glimpse of the desert creatures.

It was clear that Grandpa cherished the desert ecosystem. He continued to point out the diversity of plant and animal habitats. And although he began the hike bored, Miguel found he was growing to appreciate the desert as well. He was able to identify a desert iguana that Grandpa had talked about earlier. He gazed in astonishment at the secret hideaways of desert life.

Miguel thought all he would see today was a bunch of sand and rocks. Instead he found the wonders of the hidden desert ecosystem.

Spellings for the /o͞o/ and /oo/ Sounds

> **Focus** Many words contain the *oo* spelling. However, the words may sound different. For example, the words *soothe* and *looked* contain the same spelling, but they are pronounced differently.
>
> - /o͞o/ can be spelled oo.
>   Examples: *s*oo*the, tr*oo*ps*
>
> - /oo/ can be spelled oo.
>   Examples: *l*oo*ked, b*oo*kcase*

PRACTICE Sort the words below. Write each word under the correct heading.

choose	plywood	tools	mushroom	yearbook	soot
barefoot	adulthood	brook	waterproof	homeschool	carpool

/o͞o/ spelled oo   **/oo/ spelled oo**

1.   7.

2.   8.

3.   9.

4.   10.

5.   11.

6.   12.

APPLY Choose a word from the box to complete each sentence.

childproof	afternoon	firewood	bookshelf	bloom
woodpecker	groom	neighborhood	hardwood	igloos

13. The Inuit built _____ for shelter during the winter season.

14. A _____ is a kind of bird that digs into trees in search of insects.

15. Parents often _____ their homes to protect their young kids from harm.

16. In my _____, there are twelve homes.

17. I love to play outside each _____ when I get home from school.

18. Marissa grabbed a short story from the _____.

19. In the spring, we love to watch the flowers _____.

20. Uncle Tony brought us _____ to keep our house warm.

21. The bride and _____ happily celebrated their wedding day.

22. We have _____ floors in every room of our home.

Phonics • *Skills Practice*

Inflectional Endings -ed and -ing

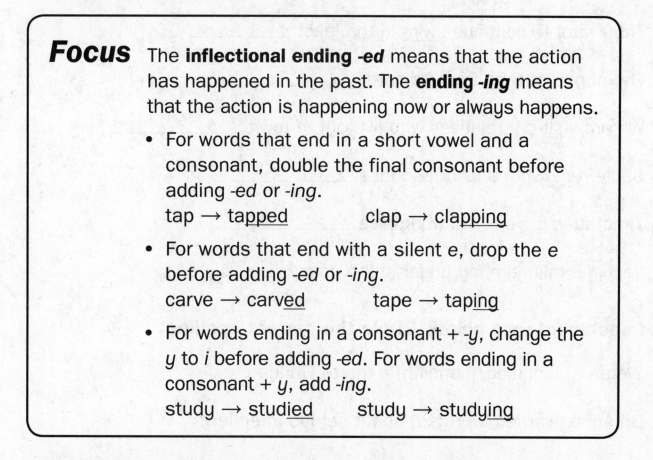

Focus The **inflectional ending -ed** means that the action has happened in the past. The **ending -ing** means that the action is happening now or always happens.

- For words that end in a short vowel and a consonant, double the final consonant before adding -ed or -ing.

  tap → ta<u>pped</u>   clap → cla<u>pping</u>

- For words that end with a silent e, drop the e before adding -ed or -ing.

  carve → carv<u>ed</u>   tape → tap<u>ing</u>

- For words ending in a consonant + -y, change the y to i before adding -ed. For words ending in a consonant + y, add -ing.

  study → stud<u>ied</u>   study → stud<u>ying</u>

PRACTICE **Read each sentence. Write *Yes* if the -ed or -ing ending has been added correctly. Write *No* if it has not.**

1. He <u>introducied</u> me to a new friend. _____

2. We are <u>skipping</u> over mud puddles. _____

3. Stacy <u>believed</u> the answer was correct. _____

4. She is <u>payeing</u> for our meal. _____

5. The sun was <u>shinning</u> brightly in the sky. _____

6. I <u>cried</u> when I heard the sad news. _____

7. Dante and I are <u>sleding</u> down the hill. _____

8. The track team is <u>training</u> for the next meet. _____

APPLY Read each sentence. Change the underlined word to the correct verb tense by adding the proper inflectional ending.

9. They want to continue <u>swim</u> in the lake. _____

10. The puppy <u>escape</u> from its yard. _____

11. We are <u>visit</u> our relatives who live out of town. _____

12. Sadie <u>reply</u> with a kind response. _____

13. Timothy is <u>drive</u> to his workplace. _____

14. I accidentally <u>jam</u> my finger in the door. _____

Read each sentence below. Circle the correct spelling.

15. We are (plannying/planning) a trip to Florida.

16. Breanna (worried/worryed) about her job interview.

17. We greeted one another by (shakeing/shaking) hands.

18. I (slippied/slipped) and fell on the icy sidewalk.

19. I am (pouring/pourring) myself a glass of lemonade.

20. My grandparents (saved/saveed) many valuables from their childhood.

21. Reed is (waiting/waitting) patiently to go to the zoo.

22. We were (permited/permitted) to play outside until 8:00 pm.

Word Analysis • *Skills Practice*

Working for the Citizens

Since ancient times, people have known the importance of a government. A government is a group of people who make decisions for a specific area. Some governments make decisions for a whole country. Some governments make decisions for a small town. In America, there are several levels of government. But no matter what level, the people that are part of the government are expected to be leaders.

In communities across the country, leaders make decisions. They get to make decision because people voted for them. The voters choose their leaders. It becomes that leader's job to manage the community the best way possible. Leaders work for the citizens. It is the government's job to make a community run smoothly.

Think about a person who wants to lead a community. That candidate tries to convince the voters that he or she will manage things better than any other candidate. The candidate makes promises to the community. The candidate shows why his or her ideas are better. Voters usually elect leaders who they feel will keep their promises, and those who have the best ideas.

For example, a candidate named Alice might promise to use tax money for a new park. If there is enough demand for that, the voters will elect Alice. The community will expect Alice to have the park built. Alice will need to balance the desire for the park with other community needs. The price of a new park has to be weighed against other costs—costs like keeping up the police and fire departments. Alice has to make choices about how the money will be spent. This can be hard. Alice must do what she thinks is best. After examining everything, Alice decides the park should be built.

Of course, Alice will not build the park herself. A leader does not work alone. She will have to hire people to do the work. Land must be bought. Money must be spent wisely. Community members must agree that Alice is planning things well. There may be a competition among citizens to sell land to the city. City workers will inspect locations. Many factors must be thought of. How large should the park be? Where should it be? What park equipment will be most popular?

Eventually Alice makes the needed decisions. The park is built and opened to the public. It is a nice place for people to relax and have fun. Adults and children enjoy going there. The community becomes a more pleasant place in which to live, because leaders and citizens worked together.

Citizens give taxes to pay for their community needs. They elect leaders to spend that money in productive ways. A good leader listens to advice from citizens. Eventually there will be another election. If Alice has managed the tax money in ways that citizens like, she may be elected again.

Spellings for the /ow/ and /ō/ Sounds

Focus Many words contain the *ow* spelling. However, the words may sound different. For example, the words *arrow* and *however* contain the same spelling, but they are pronounced differently.

- /ow/ can be spelled *ow*.
  Examples: *cl<u>ow</u>n, touchd<u>ow</u>n*

- /ow/ can be spelled *ou_*.
  Examples: *backgr<u>ou</u>nd, disc<u>ou</u>nt*

- /ō/ can be spelled *_ow*.
  Examples: *thr<u>ow</u>ing, scarecr<u>ow</u>*

PRACTICE Sort the words below. Write each word under the correct heading.

| undertow | allowance | grouchy | overthrow |
| empower | announce | rowdy | lounge |

/ow/ = ow	/ow/ = ou_	/ō/ = _ow
1. _____	4. _____	7. _____
2. _____	5. _____	8. _____
3. _____	6. _____	

APPLY Read each clue or definition below. Then select the word from the word box that matches the clue or definition. Write the word on the line.

outgrow	thousand	drowsy	accountant	homegrown
pronounce	row	vowel	Moscow	cloudy

9. To correctly say or speak a word _____

10. Something made or sold in the local area _____

11. The capital of Russia _____

12. An amount equal to ten times one hundred _____

13. To become too large for something, such as clothing

_____

14. The opposite of a consonant _____

15. Someone whose job it is to keep financial records

_____

16. To move a boat with the use of oars _____

17. Overcast and gloomy _____

18. A sleepy feeling _____

Comparatives and Superlatives

FOCUS **Comparatives** compare two nouns or verbs. **Superlatives** compare three or more nouns or verbs. Remember, *adjectives* describe *nouns*. *Adverbs* describe *verbs*. With comparatives and superlatives, the form of the adjective or adverb is changed.

- To make an adjective or adverb a comparative, add *er* for shorter words. Use the word *more* before some longer adjectives and adverbs.

  Examples: bright → bright<u>er</u>
  honest → <u>more</u> honest

- To make an adjective or adverb a superlative, add *est* for shorter words. Use the word *most* before some longer adjectives and adverbs.

  Examples: quick → quick<u>er</u> → quick<u>est</u>
  frequently → <u>more</u> frequently →
  <u>most</u> frequently

PRACTICE **Read each sentence. Circle the correct answer below.**

1. Katya is the _____ runner on the team.
   a. most fast   **b.** fastest

2. Thomas feels _____ about the test than his best friend does.
   a. nervouser   **b.** more nervous

3. Of the four puppies, Buster is the _____.
   a. thinnest   **b.** most thin

APPLY Read each sentence. Use the correct comparative or superlative form of the word in parentheses to complete the sentence. Write the word on the line.

4. I feel _____ at home than I do at school. (comfortable)

5. The oil tycoon is the _____ woman in her entire country. (rich)

6. Sidney tried the _____ of all her classmates to win the contest. (hard)

7. Liam sings _____ than David does. (gracefully)

8. This box is _____ than the last one I moved. (heavy)

9. Of the ten spelling words, Anna thought the last word was the _____. (difficult)

10. Laura and Mario are content, but Ariana is the _____ of them all. (happy)

11. For the first time ever, I awoke _____ than my little brother. (early)

12. The sun is shining _____ today than it did yesterday. (brightly)

13. Dad had to wait the _____ of anyone else to see the doctor. (long)

14. Matthew was _____ with his delicate science project than Vince was. (careful)

15. After a series of popular roles, the young actor became the _____ person in the world. (famous)

The Role of Government

What if we had no government? How would life be different? Having a government is very important. Governments provide many services for their citizens. Without a government, life would be difficult. No one would build or repair public roads. Fewer goods would be available. Clean food and water might be hard to find. If a house caught fire, there would be no one to put it out. We have a government to provide these kinds of services.

All citizens have the right to government services. A citizen is a person who is a part of a city, state, or country. Citizens must obey the laws of where they live. They also have certain rights and benefits.

In the United States, people become citizens in several ways. Anyone born in the country is a citizen. If your parents are citizens, or if you are adopted by citizens, you become one too. People born in other countries can become citizens. They must agree to support the United States Constitution.

Some of the rights of U.S. citizens are listed in the Constitution. The first ten amendments protect our basic rights. We know them as the Bill of Rights.

One right that the Bill of Rights guarantees is freedom of speech. This right means that people can say what they think, even if others do not agree. We have the freedom to practice any religion. This means that people can believe in any religion they choose. We have the right to what is called "peaceful assembly." This means that we can hold large meetings in public places.

Citizens also have the right to tell the government what they think, especially if they think they are being treated unjustly. And we have the right to choose the people who represent us. We do this by voting in elections.

While citizens have rights and freedoms, they also have many responsibilities. People must understand and obey the laws. This means knowing what is expected and allowed in your community. We must respect the role of police officers, firefighters, and other officials. We must also honor the rights of other people.

We need our government to provide services and protect our rights. But our government needs us too. We choose the people that represent us in the government. Through elections, we get to choose our leaders. If they are doing a bad job, they will not get elected again. That is how the people make sure the government is doing the best job it can.

Fluency • *Skills Practice*

Spellings for the /aw/ Sound

Focus
- /aw/ can be spelled *au_*.
  Examples: *bec<u>au</u>se, f<u>au</u>lt*

- /aw/ can be spelled *aw*.
  Examples: *s<u>aw</u>mill, j<u>aw</u>bone*

- /aw/ can be spelled *augh*.
  Examples: *distr<u>augh</u>t, t<u>augh</u>t*

- /aw/ can be spelled *ough*.
  Examples: *f<u>ough</u>t, th<u>ough</u>tful*

- /aw/ can be spelled *al*.
  Examples: *<u>al</u>so, inst<u>al</u>l*

PRACTICE **Circle the word with the correct /aw/ spelling.**

1. fraud   frawd

2. swaulow   swallow

3. thought   thaught

4. outlau   outlaw

5. awction   auction

6. daughter   doughter

7. paulm   palm

8. brawny   braughny

APPLY Read each sentence below. Find a word from the word box that can replace the underlined word or phrase. Write the word on the line.

wallet	dawn	naughtiest	lawn	granddaughter
exhausted	brawl	flaunt	bought	false

9. The information you were given is <u>not true</u>. _____

10. I felt <u>completely worn out</u> after my volleyball game. _____

11. The men involved in the <u>fight</u> were punished. _____

12. Her <u>son's little girl</u> has brown hair and brown eyes. _____

13. I helped Uncle Steve pick out a new <u>case that holds money</u>.

_____

14. Rory <u>purchased</u> a new keychain. _____

15. At <u>daybreak</u>, we took a boat ride on the river. _____

16. Drew likes to <u>show off</u> his acting skills. _____

17. Layla was the <u>worst behaved</u> student during recess.

_____

18. My dad tries to mow our <u>grass-covered yard</u> once a week.

_____

Irregular Comparatives and Superlatives

FOCUS Some **comparatives** and **superlatives** are irregular. This means they do not follow the normal rules.

- Irregular comparatives do not add *-er* or *more*. Irregular superlatives do not add *-est* or *most*.

Adjective		Comparative		Superlative
good	→	better	→	best

Adverb		Comparative		Superlative
far	→	farther	→	farthest

PRACTICE Choose a comparative adjective or adverb from the box to complete each sentence.

farther	less	worse	more	better

1. The weather was good yesterday, but today it is even _better_.

2. The milk was bad yesterday; it can only be _____ today.

3. There were many ducks on the shore, but there were still _____ on the pond.

4. The family had driven far, but they had even _____ to go on their trip.

5. I already had little energy this morning, and now I have even _____.

APPLY Choose a superlative adjective or adverb from the box to complete each sentence.

worst	farthest	least	best

6. Benny beat the other runners because he ran the _____.

7. Josh did not finish his meal because it was the _____ thing he had ever tasted.

8. The second song is better than the first, but the third is _____.

9. Of all the girls, Jan was the thirstiest because she drank the _____ all day long.

Read each group of sentences. Write a new sentence comparing the information, using at least one irregular comparative or superlative.

10. Raquel has two marbles. Zoe has three. Shea has four.

_____

_____

11. Anna ran halfway across the field. Saabir ran to the end of the field.

_____

_____

12. Trey got an A on the test. Corbin did not do as well as Trey.

_____

_____

Word Analysis • *Skills Practice*

Right to Vote: One Girl's Journal

February 21, 1919

Dear Diary, I just learned Mother will be spending July traveling the country. She is raising support for a law that lets women vote. We learned about amendments to the Constitution in school. Mother is trying to have a new amendment passed. She says, "without voting rights, people cannot be full citizens. Why shouldn't women be full citizens too?" I think she is exactly right!

June 20, 1919

Oh Diary, how lucky I feel to be part of history! Mother is going to let me go with her on her trip. Our goal is to convince other states to pass the Nineteenth Amendment. That would allow women to vote. It would treat women as equal to men.

According to the Constitution, three-fourths of states must pass it. Since there are forty-eight states, we need thirty-six to vote in our favor. That seems like a lot! But we have more than two million people helping. Many state governments are on summer break though. It has been hard to get their attention. Even harder to get their votes!

As time passes, Mother feels we might lose support. But the worst challenge comes from those against the amendment. Some people think women aren't able to make important decisions. Even some women believe this! Mother cannot explain how a woman could feel this way. I don't get it either. But I am trying to stay hopeful.

December 30, 1919

Twenty-two states have now passed the amendment. Only fourteen more to go! Mother is on another trip. She left before our school break, so I couldn't go this time. School is closed now though, so I've been reading the newspaper. I want to keep up with the latest news. I'm even making an amendment banner. With every state that passes it, I sew on a gold star. I have already made all thirty-six stars. I know we will win!

August 18, 1920

VICTORY! Mother and Father took us to the local news office. When the call finally came, everyone burst into cheers! The long fight was finally over. The dreams of so many brave women had come true.

Later, we learned how close the vote was. One voter even left the hospital to cast his vote. The final voter said he supported the amendment because his mother wanted him to.

At home this evening, we cooked a feast to celebrate. And I shared in the work equally with Mother, Father, and my brothers.

Spellings for the /oi/ Sound

> **Focus**
> - /oi/ can be spelled *oi*.
>   Examples: *checkp**oi**nt*, *br**oi**l*
> - /oi/ can be spelled *_oy*.
>   Examples: *empl**oy**ee*, *l**oy**alty*

PRACTICE **Read each word below. Circle any spellings that have the /oi/ sound as shown in the Focus box above. Cross out the word if it does not have an /oi/ sound and spelling.**

1. growing

2. turmoil

3. employed

4. worried

5. toiled

6. loaned

7. producing

8. corduroy

9. invoice

10. coy

APPLY Read each clue or definition below. Then select the word from the word box that matches the clue or definition. Write the word on the line.

alloy	disappoint	ointment	boycott
royalty	moisture	overjoyed	noisy

11. To fail to satisfy a hope or expectation

_____

12. To refuse to buy or use something as part of a protest

_____

13. A small amount of liquid that makes something wet or damp

_____

14. Members of a noble family, including a king or queen

_____

15. A lotion or similar substance which is rubbed onto the skin (often for medical purposes)

_____

16. Having a loud and possibly unpleasant sound

_____

17. A new metal created by melting and then combining two or more metals together

_____

18. Feeling extremely happy

_____

Content Words and Shades of Meaning

FOCUS
- **Content words** are specific to a topic or a subject area. They provide meanings and examples as a way of better understanding a given topic or subject area.
  Example: Think about words that are related to the topic of government.
  The word *constitution* is "a document that describes the beliefs and laws of a country." Therefore, *constitution* is a content word related to *government*.

- Words with **shades of meaning** have nearly the same definitions. However, there are slight differences in their meanings. In a set of similar words, think about which word has the stronger or more powerful shade of meaning.
  Example: *big → large → enormous*
  Large is of slightly greater size than *big*.
  Enormous is of greater size than *large*.

PRACTICE Read each set of words. Circle the content word in each set that is related to the topic of government.

1. brother   airplane   success   voting

2. amendment   language   mansion   definition

3. safety   mathematics   judicial   television

4. hurricane   representative   intelligent   cargo

APPLY Read each sentence below. Then read the definition for the missing content word located after each sentence. Complete each sentence by writing a word from the word box on the line that matches the definition.

patriotism	settlement	ballot	senator

5. The _____ drafted a new bill and proposed it to his coworkers. "a lawmaker"

6. Early colonists displayed _____ during the American Revolutionary War. "great loyalty to one's country"

7. Marena cast her _____ at the local voting station. "the action or system of voting, usually in secret"

8. The pilgrims established a new _____ along the east coast. "a place where people start a new community"

Read each pair of words. Think about the relationship of the first word to the second word. Then look at the words listed below. Circle the word that has the strongest or most powerful shade of meaning. Then write the word on the line.

9. special → extraordinary → _____

   exceptional   good   smart

10. whisper → talk → _____

    speak   yell   hesitate

11. sluggish → weak → _____

    feeble   tired   rude

12. interested → curious → _____

    available   generous   inquisitive

Word Analysis • *Skills Practice*

Being a Good Citizen

Do you enjoy living in a country where you can express your ideas? Do you look forward to the day you can vote? These are just two of the duties of an American citizen. Being a citizen means more than just living somewhere. It means accepting certain duties and responsibilities.

People who are citizens of the United States must follow laws. That is another duty of being a citizen. In America, laws are enforced by the judicial system. If people break laws, they are punished. They may be fined or imprisoned.

If people do not follow the law, they may end up in court. There, a jury will decide if they are guilty or not. Jury members are local citizens. Being on a jury is part of being a citizen. People must serve on a jury if they are called to do so.

Paying your taxes is also a responsibility of a good citizen. The money that citizens pay in taxes helps maintain the government. The money can be used in many different ways. Some of it helps pay for schools. Some of it helps keep roads and highways in good shape. Some of it is used for military needs.

Citizens have many rights. Voting is one of these rights. It allows the people to select their leaders. But voting is not only a right, it is a duty. People show that they care about their community by voting. If people did not vote in elections, the government would not function properly. Learning about political candidates and issues is part of this duty. That way, people can make smart choices when they vote.

Being a good citizen also means helping out your community. One way to do this is by volunteering. Some people volunteer to build houses for those who need them. Others collect food and clothing. Volunteers help make their community a better place. They set up recycling programs. They keep streets and parks clean.

American citizenship is about more than having responsibilities though. Most people consider it a privilege to live in America. That is because Americans have so many freedoms. There are lots of countries in the world that are not free. People come from all around the world to live in America. They hope to one day become citizens too.

Being a United States citizen is an important job. Good citizens take it seriously. They respect the ideas that formed America. They respect each other. Good citizens take pride in helping their community succeed.

Spellings for the /ō/, /ū/, /o͞o/, and /ow/ Sounds

Focus Review the following sounds and spellings:

- /ō/ can be spelled _ow.
  Example: elb*ow*

- /ū/ can be spelled u_e, _ew, and _ue.
  Examples: contrib*ute*, f*ew*, resc*ue*

- /o͞o/ can be spelled _ue, _ew, and u_e.
  Examples: s*ued*, cash*ew*, excl*ude*

- /ow/ can be spelled ow.
  Example: br*ow*se

PRACTICE Read each word below. Circle *Yes* if it has an /ō/, /ū/, /o͞o/, or /ow/ sound and spelling as shown in the Focus box above. Circle *No* if the word does not have any of these sounds and spellings.

1. trooper   Yes   No

2. powder   Yes   No

3. world   Yes   No

4. miscue   Yes   No

5. consume   Yes   No

6. devote   Yes   No

7. fellow   Yes   No

8. withdrew   Yes   No

APPLY Read each pair of words. Circle the correct spelling.

9. nephue   **nephew**

10. **argue**   argew

11. croun   **crown**

12. **absolute**   absolewte

Read the rough draft of the paragraph below. Cross out the six spelling errors. Write the correct spellings above the crossed-out words.

Today we went to the amuesment park. As we drove to the park, Shayna noticed a fue clouds. She said, "I hope it does not start raining. That will ruin our plans." I assewmed the weather would be fine, so I replied, "There are only a couple clouds. I would not worry about it." After going on only two rides, however, I felt some raindrops. This was followed by houwling winds, which was another cluhe that a thunderstorm was approaching. That is when we decided to run to the nearby shelter area. Since we could not go on anymore rides, Shayna's parents had the great idea to join in a barbecew with another group of people. We were a little disappointed, but the day turned out quite nicely. We met new friends and enjoyed great food. As soon as we were done eating, the storm ended and a rainbow appeared in the sky!

Words with the Same Base

> ***Focus*** **Words with the same base** belong to a family
> of words. When you add affixes or inflectional
> endings to a base word, the word's meaning or
> tense changes. Sometimes, the part of speech
> changes as well.
>
> • *Decide* is a base word. Other words that have the
> same base word as *decide* are *undecided* and
> *decision*. *Undecided* is an adjective that means
> "not yet made a choice" and contains a prefix
> and an inflectional ending. *Decision* is a noun
> that means "a choice that has been made after
> consideration" and contains a suffix.
>
> Example: **Base word → success**
> Words with the same base
> *success → success<u>ful</u>, success<u>fully</u>, <u>un</u>success<u>ful</u>*

PRACTICE **Read the words from the word box. Then
look at the base words and the blank spaces below. Add a
beginning or ending (or both) to each base word to form a
word from the word box. Then write the word on the line.**

| replace | undependable | believable |

1. _____ + depend + _____ = _____

2. _____ + place = _____

3. believe – e + _____ = _____

APPLY Read each sentence. Look at the underlined base word. Circle the new word that comes from the same underlined base word that correctly completes each sentence.

4. Radha thought the painting was the most <u>interest</u> piece at the museum.

   disinterest   interested   interesting

5. Our dog is <u>fright</u> by the new baby.

   frightful   frightened   frightening

6. I will not tolerate being treated with <u>respect</u>.

   disrespect   respectful   respects

7. Graham has a very pleasant and <u>like</u> personality.

   unlikely   likable   liked

8. We used the subway as our means of <u>transport</u>.

   transported   transportation   transporting

9. Manuel began to experience some <u>comfort</u> after sitting on the plane for six hours.

   discomfort   uncomfortable   comforting

10. I hope to <u>create</u> the same drawing as the one I made in art class last week.

    recreate   creating   creation

Fluency Checklist

As you read the following poem, be sure to keep these things in mind to help you read with the appropriate rate, accuracy, and expression.

As you read, make sure you

☐ pause longer at a period or other ending punctuation.

☐ raise your voice at a question mark.

☐ use expression when you come to an exclamation point.

☐ pause at commas but not as long as you would at a period.

☐ think of the character and how he or she might say his or her words whenever you come to quotation marks.

☐ remember not to read so fast that someone listening could not hear the individual words or make sense of what is being read.

☐ stop and reread something that does not make sense.

Election Day

Today it is election day,
and at the polls we're free
to cast a vote and celebrate
our democracy.

Today we'll exercise a right
that our forefathers wrote.
The future of this nation
still depends on every vote.

Are you ready? Now it's time
to make a careful choice.
Today it is election day,
a day to use your voice.

A Most Unusual Tea Party

"Where are we going?" Samuel asked. He could see his breath in the December night air.

Dad replied, "We are going to Boston Harbor. I do not want you to miss what will happen there tonight."

Sam forgot about the cold. "What do you mean?" he asked excitedly.

"Have you heard the people complain about taxation without representation?" Dad asked.

"Yes," said Sam.

"Do you know what that means?" asked Dad.

"Not exactly," admitted Sam.

"Who is in charge of the colonies?" prompted Dad.

"Britain," said Sam quickly.

"Yes, the British government makes our laws," Dad went on. "That includes deciding what taxes we pay. We do not get to help pick our leaders and we do not get to help decide what laws and taxes are fair to us. We have no representation in Britain. We have been angry about this for a long time. The Tea Act that Britain passed this year has made things worse."

"That is taxation without representation, right?" said Sam.

Dad smiled, "Yes, good for you, I am glad you understand."

"It is unfair that the colonies have no one to represent them when the British make these laws," said Sam.

"Exactly," agreed Dad. "The British taxed our tea, so to protest that, we stopped drinking it."

"It seems like we sacrificed our daily cup of tea for a good cause," smiled Sam.

"We tried to get tea from other places," said Dad, "but the British stopped us. That brings us to tonight."

Sam noticed that they were at the harbor. He could see the tall ships docked nearby and crowds of people quietly gathered on the docks.

Sam listened to those around him. "People are talking about independence for the colonies and an American government," Sam whispered.

Dad nodded. "I told you that people are restless. They want change and tonight we will see a major protest. Hopefully this will help set things right."

Dad pointed to the ships. "Look," he said.

As Sam watched, men appeared on three ships. The crowd stirred as the men began dropping crates into the sea.

"What are they doing?" asked Sam.

"Those are the Sons of Liberty dumping tea into the harbor."

The crowd roared its approval and Sam whooped in delight.

The Sons of Liberty dumped 342 crates of British tea into the harbor.

"Now the British will listen," Sam declared.

"I think tonight will be remembered as the most unusual tea party in history," said Dad.

They walked home filled with hope for a bright future.

Common Sense

Thomas Paine was one of the most important voices of the American Revolution. He wrote a booklet called *Common Sense.* In it, Paine said the colonies should set up their own government and rule themselves.

Thomas Paine was born in Britain in 1737. As he grew up, he began to develop a lot of ideas and write down some of his thoughts. In 1774, Paine met Benjamin Franklin in London. Franklin encouraged and helped Paine move to Philadelphia. Paine probably learned a lot about the trouble between the American colonies and Britain by spending time with Franklin.

Meanwhile, those troubles were growing. The American colonies did not like being taxed by Britain. The colonies did not want to give Britain their money. They had no voice in the British government.

In 1775, the Americans and British fought their first battle. The American Revolution had begun!

Nobody knew what was going to happen if the Americans won. Not everyone on the colonies even wanted to be free from British rule. Paine had ideas about what the Americans should do. He wrote the answers in *Common Sense,* which was published in 1776. What did Paine write about in *Common Sense*?

He said the colonies did not gain anything by being connected to Britain. First, Britain was a small island. How could an island rule a continent? In addition, not all of the colonists were British. People from all over Europe had moved to the colonies. Paine also argued that Britain was too far away. It took too long for important news to travel back and forth.

In his booklet, Paine wrote that he had used "simple facts, plain arguments, and common sense." The title of the book came from those words. People who were loyal to Britain and the king attacked the ideas in *Common Sense.* But on both sides, everyone paid attention to the book.

Next, Paine wrote booklets called *The American Crisis*. General George Washington gave these booklets to his troops. The soldiers were tired and hungry. There was not enough money to feed and clothe them. Paine's words encouraged the soldiers to keep fighting. In 1781, the British commander surrendered his Army. America had won!

When the French Revolution broke out not much later, Paine wrote in support of the people and moved to France. In 1802, Paine moved back to the United States. He was not as popular now and when he died in 1809, he was both poor and lonely. In 1776, however, his ideas helped Americans support the fight for independence.

Suffixes -y and -ly

FOCUS A **suffix** is a word part added to the end of a base word. The suffix **-y** means "full of" and can be added to some nouns.

- The suffix -y changes a noun into an adjective.
  chill ("cold") → **a chilly night** (Ex: *a cold night*)
- If the word ends in e, drop the final e before adding -y.
  shade → **shady**
- In most cases, double a consonant before adding -y.
  mud → **muddy**

The suffix **-ly** means "in a certain way" and can be added to some adjectives.

- The suffix -ly changes an adjective into an adverb. Remember, an adverb is a word that describes a verb, an adjective, or another adverb.
  light ("not heavy") → **skip lightly** ("skip in a light way")
- If the base word ends in y, change the y to i before adding -ly.
  happy → **happily**

PRACTICE Read each -ly or -y word below. Write the base word on the line.

1. wildly _____

2. noisy _____

3. deeply _____

4. quietly _____

5. dirty _____

6. lucky _____

7. necessarily _____

8. foggy _____

APPLY **Read each sentence below. Complete the definition of the underlined word.**

9. "I won't go!" she said <u>loudly</u>.

   Loudly means to do something in a _____ way.

10. Pat <u>gently</u> picked up the puppy.

    Gently means to do something in a _____ way.

11. The mother spoke to her children about their <u>dirty</u> room.

    Dirty means full of _____.

12. He shook his head <u>sadly</u>.

    Sadly means to do something in a _____ way.

13. The old car looked broken and <u>rusty</u>.

    Rusty means full of _____.

14. The <u>needy</u> cat meowed for Dana's attention.

    Needy means full of _____.

Read the paragraph below. Find four mistakes the writer made when spelling words with the suffixes -ly and -y. Cross them out and write the correct spellings above them.

Recently, scientists studied a sanddy rock. They figured out that this rock used to be part of Mars. It flew quietily through space until it hit Earth. What was important, however, was that this rock had curvey holes in it. On Earth, small living things make holes in rocks. Could there have been life on Mars? It will take years to know if there realy was life on Mars.

Word Analysis • *Skills Practice*

Latin Suffixes *-ment* and *-ive*

FOCUS The Latin suffix **-ment** can be added to some verbs and means "action" or "process."

- The suffix *-ment* turns a verb into a noun.
  pay ("to give what is owed") → **payment** ("the action of paying")

The Latin suffix **-ive** can be added to some verbs and nouns and means "inclined to" or "likely to."

- The suffix *-ive* turns a verb into an adjective.
  defend ("to protect") → **defen<u>sive</u>** ("likely to to protect")
- If the word ends in *e*, drop the *e* and add *-ive*.
  decora<u>te</u> → **decorat<u>ive</u>**
- If the word ends in *de*, change the *de* to *s* before adding *-ive*.
  conclu<u>de</u> → **conclu<u>sive</u>**

PRACTICE Read each word with the Latin suffix *-ment* or *-ive* below. Write the base word on the line.

1. recruitment _____

2. impressive _____

3. encouragement _____

4. progressive _____

5. employment _____

6. narrative _____

7. retirement _____

8. effective _____

APPLY Add the Latin suffix *-ment* to each word in the boxes below. Use the new word to complete the sentence.

9. | arrange | They made an _____ to meet after lunch.

10. | entertain | The concert was great _____.

11. | refresh | Mom set out apple juice as a _____.

12. | settle | The colonists created a new _____.

13. | achieve | My best _____ is my science award.

Add the Latin suffix *-ive* to each word in the boxes below. Use the new word to complete the sentence.

14. | persuade | I wrote a _____ paper on the need to protect wildlife.

15. | create | The story had a very _____ plot.

16. | cooperate | The students were asked to be _____ during the exam.

17. | innovate | My employer is looking for fresh, _____ ideas.

18. | appreciate | I was very _____ of his kindness.

Word Analysis • *Skills Practice*

We Can Rebuild!

Jordan awoke to the blaring cry of the city's emergency sirens. "Grab some clothes," his mother said calmly. "The hurricane is coming."

Jordan jumped up and looked out the window into the darkness. He could hear crashing waves coming from the sea.

With a few necessities in hand, Jordan's family rushed to the car. The neighbors were packing up too.

In the car, the radio announced the news: the storm was a category four out of five. They had named it Morris, and it was moving fast. The hurricane could hit land in less than eight hours, so the highway was jammed with traffic leaving the city.

"Evacuate," the radio said. "Get to higher ground." Jordan's family was doing just that!

Later, from the safety of a hotel, they watched the storm on television. The winds looked fierce and had blown trees down. The reporters said that the city was flooding. Storm water was filling the city and rushing through the streets. *What would happen to our home?* Jordan worried.

Two days later, Jordan and his family could at last go home. They drove back down the highway. When they got to the city, they saw buildings in ruin and many streets still flooded. The storm had damaged the entire city.

When they got to their street, they hardly recognized it. Wind and flood water had ripped away the trees. The storm had toppled walls, ripped off roofs, and flooded homes.

Mr. Miller, a neighbor, walked up to Jordan's family and sighed. "I'm leaving," he said. "I'll find another home far from the coast, where hurricanes can't touch me."

"I understand," Jordan's father answered. "The city wasn't prepared for such a strong storm."

"This could happen again next year," Mr. Miller continued. "And next time it could be even worse."

Jordan did not like what he heard. "Other cities have had hurricanes too," he said. "There have been tornados and floods and fires. And they've rebuilt and made things better. We can do that too!"

Jordan's father agreed. "They are learning to predict storms sooner so they can warn people."

"They're making safer homes," Jordan's mother added. "Builders can make 'stormproof' homes. They will be sturdy and withstand high winds."

Jordan's family decided to not move away; they would stay and rebuild their home. Jordan was glad. He told his sisters there would be a lot of work to do, but they would have help. "That's what people do when weather disasters happen," he said. "We help each other. We rebuild. We will make things better!"

Suffixes -ful and -less

FOCUS A **suffix** is a word part added to the end of a base word. The suffix **-ful** can be added to some nouns and verbs and means "full of."

- The suffix -ful changes words into adjectives.
  sorrow ("sadness") → **sorrow<u>ful</u>** ("full of sadness")

The suffix **-less** can be added to some nouns and means "without" or "lacking."

- The suffix -less changes a noun into an adjective.
  worth → **worth<u>less</u>**

For both suffixes, if the base word ends in *y*, change the *y* to *i* before adding the suffix.

pity → **piti<u>ful</u>** → **piti<u>less</u>**

PRACTICE Correctly add -ful to each word below.

1. hurt _____

2. help _____

3. shame _____

4. use _____

Correctly add -less to each word below.

5. breath _____

6. effort _____

7. clue _____

8. tire _____

APPLY Read each sentence below. The definition of each missing word is shown in parentheses. Complete the sentence by writing the correct word with the suffix -*ful* or -*less* on the line.

9. Although I have to go to the dentist, the process should be
_____. ("without pain")

10. Nina chose a _____ bedspread. ("full of color")

11. It was a _____ night, and I feel exhausted this
morning. ("without sleep")

12. Kai is training to become a _____ ballerina.
("full of grace")

13. I am worried that this project will be quite _____.
("full of stress")

14. The 400-year-old painting is so valuable that it is _____.
("not having a price")

**Write a word ending in the suffix -*less* that means the
opposite of each word below.**

15. harmful _____

16. joyful _____

17. thankful _____

18. careful _____

19. powerful _____

20. fearful _____

Latin Suffixes -able and -ity

FOCUS The Latin suffix **-able** can be added to verbs or nouns and means "can be."

- The suffix -able changes a verb or noun into an adjective.
  avoid ("to stay away from") → **avoidable** ("able to be avoided")
- For most base words ending in e, drop the e before adding -able.
  debate → **debatable**

The Latin suffix **-ity** can be added to some adjectives and means "state of being."

- The suffix -ity changes an adjective into a noun.
  absurd ("foolish") → **absurdity** ("the state of being very foolish")
- If the base word ends in e, drop the e before adding -ity.
  fragile → **fragility**

PRACTICE Add the given suffix to each base word below. Write the new word and the meaning of the new word on the lines.

Word	Suffix	New Word	New Meaning
1. diverse	-ity	_____	_____
2. excite	-able	_____	_____
3. misery	-able	_____	_____
4. popular	-ity	_____	_____

APPLY **Write sentences using two of the words you generated in the Practice section.**

5. _____

_____

6. _____

_____

Think about each word's meaning. Circle the word that correctly completes each sentence below.

7. Animals at the zoo are kept in _____, but they are treated well.

   a. remarkable   **b.** captivity

8. Vaccines provide protection against _____ diseases.

   a. preventable   **b.** festivity

9. Rohan promised that his actions were _____.

   a. obesity   **b.** explainable

10. Amaya likes to be different, and she celebrates her _____.

    a. individuality   **b.** disposable

11. The company had a very _____ year.

    a. profitable   **b.** curiosity

12. My brother's accomplishments are _____.

    a. brutality   **b.** admirable

Word Analysis • *Skills Practice*

Lightning Safety

Lightning has fascinated people throughout history, including Benjamin Franklin. Franklin was a founder of the United States. He was also a community leader, a writer, and an inventor. In the 1700s Franklin began thinking about lightning.

Franklin was the first scientist in America to study lightning seriously. He wanted to understand how it could destroy buildings, and sometimes take lives. In 1752, he invented the lightning rod. A lightning rod is made of metal, usually copper. It is attached to the highest point of a building. These high points are the most likely to attract lightning. The rod acts to guide the lightning. It forces the electric current to the ground instead of the building. Franklin's invention is still used today. It saves buildings during dangerous storms. More importantly, it saves the people inside.

To show how a lightning rod worked, Franklin built a model house. He called it the Thunder House. Gunpowder was placed inside. Then Franklin touched a mini lightning rod on top with an electric current. The electricity moved downward into the ground. Nothing happened. Then he removed the lightning rod. The electricity made the powder explode. Thunder House had its roof blown off!

Years later, people had still not learned much more about lightning. The technology for understanding it did not yet exist. Today though, scientists have much better ways to study lightning.

Many lightning researchers work in Florida. It is a natural hot spot for storms and lightning. But studying natural lightning is very difficult. It is nearly impossible to predict where it will hit. Scientists can make artificial lightning indoors, but it is very expensive.

Instead, they shoot rockets at thunderclouds to study lightning! When a storm begins, they take cover in a protected trailer. Then they shoot off a special rocket. It is designed to trigger lightning when it reaches a cloud. When the rocket is hit by lightning, they can record all kinds of information.

But the researchers are careful to stay safe when working. They remain inside the special trailer. They use tools that do not attract lightning. By studying lightning, they are able to help others stay safe during a storm.

Our understanding of lightning grows every day. Franklin's lightning rod was just the beginning. Today's researchers are learning even more about how lightning works. They are also learning how dangerous lightning can be. The more we know about it, the more we can understand how to stay safe, and perhaps even harness its power someday.

Suffixes *-ion/-tion/-sion* and *-al*

FOCUS A **suffix** is a word part added to the end of a base word. The suffix *-ion/-tion/-sion* can be added to some verbs and means "action" or "process." The spelling of the suffix depends on the spelling of the base word.

- The suffix *-ion/-tion/-sion* is added to verbs to make them nouns.
  inspect ("to look carefully") → **inspect<u>ion</u>** ("the action of looking carefully at something")
  The suffix *-al* can be added to some nouns and verbs and means "of" or "relating to."
- The suffix *-al* is added to nouns and verbs to change them into adjectives.
  logic ("a reasonable way of thinking") → **logic<u>al</u>** ("having to do with logic and reasoning")

PRACTICE Combine each given base word and suffix. Write the word on the line.

1. direct   +   *-ion*   = _____

2. complete   +   *-ion*   = _____

3. culture   +   *-al*   = _____

4. subtract   +   *-ion*   = _____

5. accident   +   *-al*   = _____

6. invade   +   *-sion*   = _____

APPLY Complete each sentence by writing a word from the Practice section on the line.

7. I made an _____ mistake on my test.

8. The festival included _____ traditions from Mexico.

9. In math class, we learned _____ before multiplication.

10. Which _____ do we take after we turn right at the stop sign?

Read the paragraph below. Find six mistakes the writer made when spelling words with the suffixes *-ion/-tion/ -sion* or *-al*. Cross them out, and write the correct spellings above them.

In the 1800s, public educasion in the United States was much different than it is now. Depending on their locattion, most students attended school only a few months each year. They learned reading, writing, handwriting, and good manners. Most students did not attend school beyond the age of fourteen. When they were not in class, kids were expected to work on their family farms. This was known as agriculturel work. Because families had many children and much work to do, it was more important that the kids work rather than learn.

By the early 1900s, a politicall movement had taken hold of the nation. With this new transformttion, lawmakers realized the need for all children to have equal access to schooling. Students began attending school nine months a year. The goal was to have as many students as possible go to school from kindergarten through high school. After completing the final year of school, students received diplomas at a graduateion ceremony.

Word Analysis • *Skills Practice*

Multiple-Meaning Words

FOCUS **Multiple-meaning words** are words that share the same spellings but have different meanings. They may or may not have different pronunciations. Use a dictionary to determine if a word is a multiple-meaning word.

Example: **conduct**

conduct (kən dəkt')   *conduct* (kon' dəkt)
conduct "to lead or direct"   *conduct* "how a
                                                        person behaves"

PRACTICE **Read each sentence. Circle the correct definition for the underlined word, based on the context of the sentence.**

1. My favorite <u>state</u> to visit is Colorado.
   a. to express in speech or writing   **b.** a territory within a country

2. The workers went on <u>strike</u> after their pay was reduced.
   a. a protest organized   **b.** to hit one's body part
      by employees   against something

3. Jamie, the babysitter, will <u>watch</u> us while our parents go out for the evening.
   a. to carefully observe   **b.** a timepiece worn on the wrist

4. Kamal turned <u>right</u> onto Fallingwell Street.
   a. true or correct   **b.** a direction; the opposite of left

5. The toddler shrieked in delight as she was pushed on the <u>swing</u>.
   a. to cause to move back   **b.** a movable seat found on a
      and forth   playground

6. During math class, we learned about a new <u>figure</u> called an octagon.
   a. a shape, such as   **b.** a person's bodily shape
      a triangle or square

APPLY Read each riddle below. Write the word from the word box that solves each riddle. Each word will be used twice.

minor	patient	pitcher

7. I am calm and forgiving. What am I? _____

8. When you tip me to the side, lemonade will come pouring out. What am I? _____

9. I am not very important or valuable. What am I? _____

10. My goal is to strike out the batter. What am I? _____

11. You will find me in a doctor's office, as sick as can be. What am I? _____

12. I am under the age of eighteen. What am I? _____

Read each sentence. Write a definition for each underlined multiple-meaning word based on the context of the sentence.

13. Sentence 1: Dahlia began to <u>mold</u> the clay for her art project.

    Sentence 2: Mom said, "Clean the bathroom, so that <u>mold</u> does not begin growing."

    _____

    _____

14. Sentence 1: Ms. Langley will <u>train</u> her dance team in preparation for the competition.

    Sentence 2: The line of cars waited five minutes for the <u>train</u> to go by.

    _____

    _____

Word Analysis • *Skills Practice*

Fluency Checklist

As you read the following poem, be sure to keep these things in mind to help you read with the appropriate rate, accuracy, and expression.

As you read, make sure you

☐ pause longer at a period or other ending punctuation.

☐ raise your voice at a question mark.

☐ use expression when you come to an exclamation point.

☐ pause at commas but not as long as you would at a period.

☐ think of the character and how he or she might say his or her words whenever you come to quotation marks.

☐ remember not to read so fast that someone listening could not hear the individual words or make sense of what is being read.

☐ stop and reread something that does not make sense.

Signs of Spring

Finally, the signs of spring!
The snow has melted from the lawn.
The cherry trees are budding green
now that the glassy ice is gone.

Remember when, like gingerbread,
the houses were all frosted white?
Winter is behind us now.
The sun is shining, warm and bright.

The cherry trees will lose their blossoms
when the winds of April blow.
Tiny petals, soft and white,
will fall just like a springtime snow.

Suffixes -*ness* and -*er*

FOCUS A **suffix** is a word part added to the end of a base word. The suffix **-ness** can be added to some adjectives and means "state of being."

- The suffix -*ness* changes a word—usually an adjective—into a noun.

  dark ("having no light") → **dar<u>kness</u>** ("the state of having no light")

- If the base word ends in *y*, change the *y* to *i* before adding -*ness*.

  empt<u>y</u> → **empt<u>iness</u>**

The suffix -**er** can be added to some verbs and means "someone or something who" does something.

- The suffix -*er* changes a verb into a noun.

  lead ("to guide") → **lea<u>der</u>** ("one who helps to guide other people")

- If the base word ends in *e*, drop the *e* and add -*er*.

  manag<u>e</u> → **manag<u>er</u>**

PRACTICE Read each word with the suffix -*ness* or -*er* below. Write the base word on the line.

1. broadcaster _____

2. craziness _____

3. quickness _____

4. bowler _____

5. massiveness _____

6. hunter _____

7. sickness _____

8. painter _____

APPLY Read each sentence below. The definition of each missing word is shown in parentheses. Complete the sentence by writing the correct word with the suffix *-ness* or *-er* on the line.

9. Some people think the _____ of lemons tastes unpleasant. ("the state of being bitter")

10. Gemma loved the _____ of the newly-washed laundry. ("the state of being fresh")

11. The company hired a _____ to create its new website. ("one who designs")

12. Some campers stayed in their cabins due to the _____ of the night hike. ("the state of being dark")

13. Marissa asked for _____ after she broke the vase. ("the state of forgiving")

14. Ernest Shackleton was an _____ who made three trips to Antarctica in the early 1900s. ("one who explores")

15. My older brother is learning to become a _____. ("one who drives")

16. I enjoy the _____ of my pillows. ("the state of being smooth")

17. Aaron is a _____ of an apartment in Chicago. ("one who rents")

18. The extreme _____ of the lights gave me a headache. ("the state of being bright")

19. Tania worked as an _____ to translate Spanish into English. ("one who interprets")

20. The _____ could throw the ball faster than anyone in his league. ("one who pitches")

Content Words and Words with the Same Base

FOCUS
- **Content words** are specific to a topic or a subject area. They provide meanings and examples as a way of better understanding a given topic or subject area.
  Example: A *squall* is "a sudden, violent storm." Therefore, *squall* is a content word related to *weather*.
- **Words with the same base** belong to a family of words. When you add a prefix or suffix (or both) to a base word, the word's meaning changes. Sometimes, the part of speech changes as well.
  Example: **brave** ("courageous")
  Words with the same base as *brave* →
  brav<u>ed</u>, brav<u>est</u>, brav<u>ery</u>

PRACTICE Read each set of words. Circle the content word in each set that is related to the topic of weather.

1. banker   cyclone   vacation   lifeguard

2. hospital   emergency   meteorologist   radio

Circle the words that belong to the same base word family in each row. Then write the base word on the line.

3. reuse   uncle   misuse   _____

4. agreement   disagree   meeting   _____

5. preparation   unprepared   preparedness   _____

APPLY Read each sentence below. Then read the definition for the missing content word located under each sentence. Complete each sentence by writing a word from the word box on the line.

seasons	precipitation	forecast	fog

6. Rainforests get more _____ than most other ecosystems.

"water that falls to the ground in the form of rain, snow, or sleet"

7. There are four _____: winter, spring, summer, and autumn.

"four specific time periods during a year marked by different patterns of weather"

8. It was very hard to see through the dense _____.

"particles of water floating near ground level, which creates a hazy effect"

9. The weather _____ suggested lots of sun and warm temperatures for the next five days.

"a prediction made about the weather after studying given data and information"

Read each sentence. Change the underlined word to a word from the same base word family that makes sense in the sentence. Write the word on the line.

10. Mr. Ackerman is teaching us _divide_ rules. _____

11. That was a very _usual_ and strange story. _____

12. The _settle_ came to America seeking new opportunities and religious freedom. _____

13. It would be _wise_ of you to take bad advice. _____

14. He _save_ any important documents and threw the other ones out.

_____

15. We read the _direct_ on the side of the box. _____

Surviving the Flood

The city of Galveston is on an island off the coast of Texas. On September 8, 1900, a hurricane hit. It caused a massive flood that devastated the city. In this fiction piece, Ally Mae writes a letter to her family after the storm.

Dear Mother and Father,

I'm sure by now you have heard about the hurricane that hit Galveston. Much of the city is ruined. Thankfully Aunt Elizabeth, Uncle Richard, and I are alive.

I'm glad we don't live near the beach. The storm destroyed most of those homes, including my friend Julia's house. Julia and her family are okay though.

Last week we heard about a hurricane in Cuba. There were warnings it was moving this way. I was worried, but no one else seemed alarmed. Julia invited me to spend the afternoon at her house. Uncle Richard took me over there on his way to work. He intended to visit some patients and return for me later.

As the storm blew in, Julia did not seem concerned. She said her family was used to hurricanes. Since she wasn't worried, I tried not to be either. When Uncle Richard came back, though, he said we had to hurry home. Water was flooding through the streets. The wind blew in our faces as we raced home.

When we reached the house, we saw that the water had risen halfway up the porch. Inside, we saw the house was filled with people who had fled their homes. Aunt Elizabeth welcomed in anyone seeking shelter.

"What if the water keeps rising?" I asked.

"We will take refuge upstairs," Uncle Richard answered calmly.

The water did keep rising. Soon it was a foot deep on the living room floor. Everyone retreated upstairs. We all gathered in a bedroom. Rain was beating against the windows. The wind was blowing furiously outside.

As night fell, I stood near a window, straining to see outside. In a flash of lightning, I saw a frightening sight. The surface of the floodwater was covered with the wreckage of destroyed houses. I was glad we were all safe inside.

Thankfully, around 10:00, the floodwaters started to recede. Soon after midnight the raging wind calmed too. The nightmare was almost over.

At sunrise, we saw that Galveston was in ruins. Sadly, the flood had swept away Julia's house. But her family was safe with us. We are fortunate that we were unharmed.

Much love,

Ally Mae

The people of Galveston quickly began to rebuild. They built a seawall to hold back floodwater. It would protect them in the future. Today, Galveston is thriving, just as it was before the storm.

Greek Roots *ast*, *graph*, *log*, and *scop*

FOCUS **Roots** are word parts that have meaning. Knowing **Greek roots** can help you understand new words.

- The root **ast** means "star." It is used in words such as <u>ast</u>ronaut.
- The root **graph** means "write." It is used in words such as auto<u>graph</u>.
- The root **log** means "word" or "study." It is used in words such as dia<u>log</u>ue.
- The root **scop** means "see." It is used in words such as tele<u>scop</u>e.

PRACTICE **Look for the Greek root inside each word below. Connect each word to its meaning.**

1. asteroid

2. microscope

3. autograph

4. monologue

5. asterisk

6. biology

7. telegraph

8. astronaut

a. a tool used to look at small things

b. a star-shaped symbol

c. a small rock orbiting a star

d. a person's handwritten name

e. a speech in a play that is spoken by one person

f. a tool for communicating over long distances

g. a person who navigates space

h. the study of living things

APPLY Circle the word in each sentence that contains a Greek root. Use context clues to figure out the word's meaning. Circle the correct definition.

9. The astronomer spent a lot of time watching the night sky.

   a. a person who studies writing

   b. a person who studies stars

10. Madeline bought a new camera for her photography class.

    a. the process of making pictures with a camera

    b. the study of making speeches

11. The actor gave a prologue before the play.

    a. a speech given by an actor at the beginning of a play

    b. a person who examines plays

12. When I looked through the telescope, I could see Saturn's rings.

    a. a tool for seeing faraway things

    b. a tool that helps you write

13. People used to send messages over telegraph wires.

    a. a machine that sends photographs over long distances

    b. a machine that sends written messages over long distances

14. Pencils are made of a substance called graphite.

    a. a material used for writing

    b. a tool that helps you examine things

Word Analysis • *Skills Practice*

Latin Roots *grat*, *mar*, *miss*, and *port*

FOCUS **Roots** are word parts that have meaning. Knowing **Latin roots** can help you understand new words.

- The root **grat** means "pleasing." It is used in words such as <u>grat</u>eful.
- The root **mar** means "sea." It is used in words such as <u>mar</u>ine.
- The root **miss** means "send." It is used in words such as <u>miss</u>ion.
- The root **port** means "carry." It is used in words such as <u>port</u>able.

PRACTICE **Read each word and its meaning. Circle the Latin root inside it. Write the root's meaning.**

1. **congratulated** ("to have told people you are happy for them")
_____

2. **transport** ("to move something from one place to another')
_____

3. **mission** ("a special job a person is sent to finish") _____

4. **marine** ("relating to the sea") _____

5. **support** ("to help") _____

6. **marina** ("a small harbor for boats") _____

APPLY Use words from the previous page to complete each sentence below.

7. In 1998, a spacecraft was sent to _____ cameras and other machines to Mars.

8. The spacecraft's _____ was to find out about the history of water on Mars.

9. If Mars once had water, then it might have had _____ bacteria. These are small things that live in water.

10. People back on Earth worked to _____ the mission and guide the spacecraft.

11. Other scientists _____ these people for their good work.

Use three of the words from the previous page in sentences of your own.

12. _____

_____

13. _____

_____

14. _____

_____

Fluency Checklist

As you read the following poem, be sure to keep these things in mind to help you read with the appropriate rate, accuracy, and expression.

As you read, make sure you

☐   pause longer at a period or other ending punctuation.

☐   raise your voice at a question mark.

☐   use expression when you come to an exclamation point.

☐   pause at commas but not as long as you would at a period.

☐   think of the character and how he or she might say his or her words whenever you come to quotation marks.

☐   remember not to read so fast that someone listening could not hear the individual words or make sense of what is being read.

☐   stop and reread something that does not make sense.

Hurricane

I watched the rain
hammer the ground
until our street became a river
and the cars sailed by like boats.

I watched the wind
pull the roof from a house
quickly and easily,
as if taking the lid off a box.

I watched the water
rising in our house,
higher and higher,
until the furniture floated.

The water is gone now,
but I can still see
the line it left on the wall.
I will never forget.

The Santa Ana Winds

Southern California erupted into flames in the fall of 2003. Twelve devastating wildfires began across the area. In all, the fires burned an area the size of Rhode Island. Wildfires are nothing new to California residents. The fires in the fall of 2003 were among the worst ever to occur in the region though.

How did the fires spread so rapidly? The fierce Santa Ana winds were one of the causes. The Santa Ana winds are strong, hot, dry winds. They blow from the east or northeast during the fall and winter in Southern California. They created the ideal conditions for an inferno.

The Santa Ana winds begin high in the mountains along California's eastern border. They commonly reach speeds of thirty miles per hour. Sometimes they gust to over 100 miles per hour!

Besides fanning the flames of wildfires, the Santa Anas have other effects. The most obvious effect is hot, dry weather. The winds lower the humidity and raise temperatures. During the Santa Anas, plants, animals, and people all need more water.

Allergy sufferers also dread the arrival of the Santa Anas. In Southern California, the wind usually comes from the west. This Pacific Ocean breeze is fresh, cool, and free of dust and pollen. But the Santa Anas blow from the east. They carry pollen from the deserts. They stir up dust. This makes life difficult for people who have to cope with allergy symptoms.

The Santa Anas do have some positive effects though. Surfers eagerly await the winds. As waves come in from the west, the Santa Anas slow them down by blowing from the east. This creates tall waves for surfers to ride. It also gives surfers a longer ride. The winds also give divers clean, clear water. This results in excellent viewing of sea life below the surface.

Animals also use the winds. The clear water that divers enjoy also benefits the sea life. It allows algae to bloom and enrich the food chain. Fish, birds, and even whales enjoy this abundance of food.

Monarch butterflies spend the spring and summer in the mountains. When the Santa Anas begin, these beautiful insects begin to migrate. They ride the winds on their westward journey.

The Santa Ana winds are well known in California. Weather reports warn of their arrival. Although many people dislike the winds, they will continue to blow. They will fan wildfires, irritate allergies, and create hot weather. But most people will choose to live with them rather than leave the area they have grown to love.

Avalanche!

Avalanches—powerful snow slides—occur on snowy mountains. In the United States, most avalanches occur on the tall mountains of the West.

You might see a small version of an avalanche on a slanted roof. The snow may become too heavy and slide off. Or warmth from the sun may melt the snow a little and cause it to slide off. Mountain avalanches are similar, but they are dangerous. When snow begins sweeping down a mountain, it can take large rocks and trees with it. And as snow piles up quickly in winter, the risk becomes greater.

The steepness, or slope, of a mountain is important when it comes to avalanches. If a mountain is too steep, snow will not build up. It will slide off continually. If a mountain is not steep enough, snow will not slide at all. But if a mountain has just the right slope, dangerous avalanches can be common.

Each snowfall adds a new layer of snow to these slopes. Over time, the snow compresses down. The strong snow layers are thick and solid. The weak ones are fluffy and loose. If a strong layer builds up on a weak one, the snowpack becomes unstable. The weak layer caves in. This can be the start of an avalanche.

Any sudden weather change can trigger this avalanche. If snow falls very quickly, the existing snowpack does not have time to adjust to the new weight. The sudden increase in weight can trigger a slide.

Rain or a sudden rise in temperature can also do it. If the snow starts to melt, it becomes wet. Wet snow is not very stable. It is likely to slide.

Wind is also a problem. Wind can blow snow into large mounds quickly. The rapid change in weight the wind causes can trigger an avalanche.

Although weather can cause avalanches, people are most often the cause. Skiers, climbers, and snowboarders can set off avalanches. They can also get caught in those avalanches.

Luckily there are avalanche experts. They check the snowpack and study the weather. They dig holes in the snow to examine the layers. They can tell if an avalanche is likely to occur. They advise people about unsafe areas. Sometimes, they even cause an avalanche on purpose.

Controlled avalanches take place near ski areas, roads, and railroads. People leave the area. Then experts use explosives to start a slide. The idea is to set it off before it falls on its own.

There is no way to prevent avalanches, but thanks to these experts, they can hopefully be avoided.

Prefixes *re-*, *pre-*, *mis-*, and *un-*

> **FOCUS** A **prefix** is a word part added to the beginning of a base word or root.
> - The prefix *re-* means "again."
>   **build** ("to form using materials") → **rebuild** ("to build again")
> - The prefix *pre-* means "before."
>   **bake** ("to cook in an oven") → **prebake** ("to cook in an oven ahead of time")
> - The prefix *mis-* means "wrongly" or "badly."
>   **judge** ("to form an opinion about") → **misjudge** ("to form the wrong opinion about")
> - The prefix *un-* means "the opposite of."
>   **fold** ("to lay one part over another") → **unfold** ("to do the opposite of folding")

PRACTICE Read each definition below. Use the prefix *re-*, *pre-*, *mis-*, or *un-* to write a word that matches each definition.

1. "to behave badly" _____

2. "to locate again" _____

3. "made ahead of time" _____

4. "to do the opposite of pack" _____

5. "to consider again" _____

6. "to treat wrongly" _____

APPLY Combine the prefixes *re-*, *pre-*, *mis-*, or *un-* with the base words below. Write the new word on the line, then write a definition for the word.

Prefix	Word	New Word/New Meaning
7. *pre-*	game	_____
8. *mis-*	information	_____
9. *re-*	learn	_____
10. *un-*	known	_____
11. *pre-*	order	_____
12. *mis-*	understand	_____
13. *re-*	fuel	_____
14. *un-*	usual	_____

Choose two words from the Practice activity or the activity above. Use these words to write your own sentences.

15. _____

_____

_____

16. _____

_____

_____

Word Analysis • *Skills Practice*

Prefixes *con-* and *in-/im-*

FOCUS A **prefix** is a word part added to the beginning of a base word or root.

- The prefix **con-** means "with" or "together." Usually, this prefix is not added to a base word that can stand alone.
  conference ("a formal meeting in which people come together for discussion")

- The prefix **in-/im-** means "not."
  consistent ("constant or regular") →
  inconsistent ("not constant or regular") **proper** ("appropriate") → **improper** ("not appropriate")

PRACTICE Add the prefix *con-* or *in-/im-* to the base word or root word to form a word from the word box. Then write the new word on the line.

| inhumane   condense   informal   connect   immobile |

	Prefix		**Base Word/Root**	**New Word**
1.	_____	+	formal	_____
2.	_____	+	mobile	_____
3.	_____	+	dense	_____
4.	_____	+	humane	_____
5.	_____	+	nect	_____

APPLY Read each sentence. Write a word from the word box to complete each sentence.

insignificant	conform	impersonal	conspired

6. The criminals _____ to commit an illegal act.

7. While I think the new scientific findings are important, my friend thinks they are _____.

8. Some people believe that writing an electronic thank-you note is _____.

9. In order to start a new school club, we must agree to _____ to certain rules.

Think about each word's meaning. Circle the word that correctly completes each sentence below.

10. Chris is becoming very _____ with his dog, because it is constantly chewing up his clothes.

    a. impatient   **b.** consensus

11. It is very rude to be _____ of people who are different from you.

    a. condense   **b.** intolerant

12. My doctor wants me to _____ with a specialist about my sprained ankle.

    a. insecure   **b.** consult

Word Analysis • *Skills Practice*

Lost Treasure

Leon stood at the back door, looking out across the yard. It was summer break and he had a search to begin. He was certain that gold and other pirate treasure was buried right back there. A clever pirate would not bury his fortune at the shore. He would bury it inland in a place like Leon's yard. Leon planned to find the riches for himself.

He grabbed his shovel and went out the door. Leon picked a spot near an old stump and dug until his arms got tired. He was about to stop when his shovel hit something! Digging around with his hand, he grabbed the object and pulled. He pulled so hard that he fell backward!

"You dug up a root from that stump," a voice observed. Leon saw Mr. Howard peering over the fence. "That stump was a magnificent oak tree. But a fierce storm in 1952 damaged it and we had to cut it down. You know, this whole area was once covered with trees."

Leon could not believe his buried treasure was a tree root! He decided to try another section of yard. Quickly, he spotted something white. Maybe it was a pearl! Leon brushed the dirt away; it was a rock. But it was pointed and had an unusual shape.

"Do you know what kind of rock this is, Mr. Howard?" he asked.

"You've discovered an arrowhead. When I was a boy we found arrowheads all around here," Mr. Howard replied. "The Fox tribe lived and hunted here."

"Really? How old do you think it is?" Leon asked.

"It could be three hundred years old—maybe even older," Mr. Howard answered. Leon placed the arrowhead on the stump. He did not want to lose it.

The next day he dug in another spot, hoping to find his buried treasure. After a while, he found a brown bottle, but no treasure. He took the bottle to show Mr. Howard.

"That looks like an old medicine bottle," Mr. Howard said. "It's probably over a hundred years old."

"Who threw this out?" Leon asked.

"A family used to own a farm here. They probably did, before selling their land."

As Leon continued to search, he found more objects, but no treasure. One time he found a toy fire truck. He took it to Mr. Howard, who said it had been his when he was a boy. He had lost it, but now Leon had found it.

As summer ended, Mr. Howard invited Leon and his family to his home. "Leon, you've been busy this summer. Why don't you share your treasures?"

Leon was confused. He hadn't found any treasure. Then he realized what Mr. Howard meant. He shared the arrowhead and the story of the Fox tribe. He held up an oak leaf and talked about all the trees that had once grown here. The brown bottle led him to talk about the old farm. The toy truck was his personal favorite, because it reminded him of Mr. Howard.

As Leon spoke, he thought about the history of his community. He realized that he had found treasure after all.

Prefixes *ex-* and *en-/em-*

FOCUS A **prefix** is a word part added to the beginning of a base word or root.

- The prefix **ex-** means "out."
  export ("to send out goods or products to another country for sale")
- The prefix **en-/em-** means "put into or onto" or "to cause to be."
  large → **enlarge** ("to cause to be bigger")

PRACTICE Think about each word's meaning. Circle the word that correctly completes each sentence below. Then write the word on the line.

1. I do not want my pets _____ to the extreme heat, so I will keep them inside.
   a. engaged   **b.** exposed

2. My mismatched shoes and socks caused me to feel _____.
   a. expended   **b.** embarrassed

3. The city planner did not want to _____ visitors; therefore, she placed warning signs near areas of the beach that may be unsafe.
   a. endanger   **b.** embrace

4. A team of scientists will _____ a remote area of Easter Island located in the southeast Pacific Ocean.
   a. entwine   **b.** explore

APPLY Read each sentence below. Choose a word from
the word box to complete each sentence.

extinguisher	embattled	ensure	exchange

5. We will _____ that the doors are locked before
leaving the house.

6. In case of an emergency, an adult should know where the fire
_____ is located and how to use it.

7. Thad plans to _____ his new pants for a pair
that are the correct size.

8. The famously _____ city received help from
neighboring countries.

Write a short paragraph using at least four of the words from
either the Practice activity or the activity above. Circle the words,
and make sure they are spelled and used correctly.

_____

_____

_____

_____

_____

Word Analysis • *Skills Practice*

Prefixes *dis-* and *auto-*

> **FOCUS** A **prefix** is a word part added to the beginning of a base word or root.
>
> - The prefix **dis-** means "not" or "the opposite of."
>   **agree** ("to have the same opinion") → **disagree** ("to not have the same opinion")
>
> - The prefix **auto-** means "self."
>   **biography** ("a person's life story") → **autobiography** ("a biography that is self-written")

PRACTICE Read each word below. Circle the base word. Think about the meaning of the prefix and the base word, then write the word's meaning.

1. disadvantage   _____

2. disbelieve   _____

3. dishonest   _____

4. displease   _____

Match each word with its meaning below.

5. autograph   **a.** my life's story written by me

6. autopilot   **b.** a self-powered machine with four wheels made to take people places

7. automobile   **c.** a program that steers and pilots ships or spacecraft on its own

8. autobiography   **d.** someone's self-written name

APPLY Use a word from the word box to complete each
sentence below.

| dishonest | dislikes | autobiography | disagreed |
| discovered | disinterested | autograph | autopilot |

9. Katharine Hepburn, a famous actress, wrote an
_____ called *My Life*.

10. The boring television show made me feel
_____.

11. The brothers _____ over who was the better
basketball player.

12. A _____ person cannot be trusted.

13. Many modern aircraft come equipped with
_____.

14. When I opened the old box, I _____ treasures
from long ago.

15. Roller coasters scare Tracy, so she _____
them.

16. Last week, I got my favorite writer's _____.

Life on the Prairie

Millions of years ago, a sea covered the land in the middle of the United States. Slowly the sea drained away, and tall grasses grew where it had been.

When settlers came, they saw the grasses blowing in the wind. They called it a *prairie*, which is a French word for *meadow*. Year after year, there were fierce fires on the prairie. Many started when lightning struck the ground. The old, dry grasses burned and the fires spread. New grasses grew quickly again in the rich soil. New trees couldn't grow as quickly though. That is one reason why prairies have few trees.

Prairie fires were also set by Native Americans. They started fires to force wild animals to flee to places where it was easier to hunt them. For hundreds of years, many Native Americans lived in communities on the prairie. They made homes from the grasses. They wore the hides of the animals they hunted. They used what the land gave them and tried to waste nothing.

Settlers began coming to the prairie in the 1700s. Most came in wagons from the eastern states. They wanted to claim land to farm. The settlers lived by the groves of trees that had managed to survive the fires. The trees gave them shelter, and they could find firewood and lumber to build homes. They farmed the land near the trees.

At first, settlers thought the prairie soil was not fertile. After all, very few trees grew there. Soon they found that the prairie soil was rich and excellent for crops. A metal plow could cut through the long roots of the prairie grasses. Then the settlers could grow crops on acres of flat prairie land.

As stories of rich farmland spread, more settlers came to live on the prairie. They built homes from sod, or strips of grass and soil. They dug wide paths, called firebreaks, around their homes and fields. They did this to prevent the fires from burning them. The settlers battled grasshoppers, wind, dry spells, and the cold. Life on the prairie was tough.

Towns soon developed to support the prairie settlers. There were post offices, grocers, doctors, and schools. These communities had the necessities that settlers needed to live. When the railroad arrived, it became easier for towns to grow. More people could come from the east. It was easier to buy and sell goods.

Now there are many cities on the prairie. The farmland supplies food for much of the United States.

Prairie land, though, has become scarce. It once spread over forty percent of the United States. Now it takes up less than one percent. Fires are rare too, so more trees are growing. But now, people have begun to restore the prairie. They are planting prairie grass. They are making room for the wildlife that used to live there. They are restoring the land to how it looked when their communities first started.

Fluency • *Skills Practice*

Number Prefixes

FOCUS A **prefix** is a word part added to the beginning of a base or root word. **Number prefixes** are prefixes that have to do with numbers. They tell you the amount of something. Number prefixes include **uni-, bi-, tri-,** and **multi-.**

- The prefix **uni-** means "one."
  uniform ("a type of clothing worn by everyone in a group")
- The prefix **bi-** means "two."
  bisect ("to cut into two equal parts")
- The prefix **tri-** means "three."
  triplex ("a building that is divided into three parts")
- The prefix **multi-** means "many."
  multilevel ("having many different levels or floors")

PRACTICE Read each underlined word that contains a number prefix and circle the correct definition below.

1. The <u>bicentennial</u> of the United States was held on July 4, 1976.
   a. A two-year award for a major accomplishment
   b. A two-hundredth anniversary or celebration

2. The snake's skin is <u>multilayered</u>.
   a. Having many different layers
   b. Having three layers

3. I enjoyed reading the <u>trilogy</u> about people living in ancient Rome.
   a. Three novels that are related
   b. One novel that has many different themes

APPLY Read each sentence below. Replace each underlined phrase with a word from the box. Write the word on the line.

multitasking	tricycle	triathlon
biplane	union	bilingual

4. Kiyomi is <u>able to speak two languages</u>; she speaks Japanese and English. _____

5. Grandma bought a <u>three-wheeled vehicle that uses foot pedals</u> for my youngest sister. _____

6. Cole is frequently <u>doing many different tasks at once</u>.
_____

7. I have always wanted to ride in a <u>plane with two sets of wings</u>.
_____

8. Examples of nations that function as a <u>group of states or territories ruled by one government</u> include Switzerland, Canada, and the United States. _____

9. We cheered on Suzanne as she competed in the <u>athletic contest with three sporting events</u>. _____

Match each word with its meaning below.

10. trimester   **a.** having to do with many cultures

11. multicultural   **b.** to bring together as one

12. biweekly   **c.** a school year divided into three parts

13. unify   **d.** having to do with many types of media

14. multimedia   **e.** occurring every two weeks or twice a week

Location Prefixes

FOCUS A **prefix** is a word part added to the beginning of a base word or root. **Location prefixes** are prefixes that tell you where something is located or when something happened. Location prefixes include **mid-, sub-, trans-,** and **inter-**.

- The prefix **mid-** means "middle."
  midair ("middle of the air")
- The prefix **sub-** means "under."
  submarine ("under the water")
- The prefix **trans-** means "across."
  transistor ("a device that controls the electronic flow across components")
- The prefix **inter-** means "among" or "between."
  interlude ("a break between the first and second parts of an event")

PRACTICE Add a location prefix to each base word or root word so that the final word matches the definition.

1. _____ way   ("an *under*ground transportation system")

2. _____ mit   ("send *across* the airwaves")

3. _____ week   ("the *middle* of the week")

4. _____ com   ("a communications system that goes *between* rooms in a building")

5. _____ val   ("a period of time *between* events")

APPLY Write the word from the word box that matches
each definition below.

midday	international	transit
transform	midsummer	suburban

6. Occurring between two countries _____

7. The middle of the summer _____

8. The act of moving people or things across places _____

9. Towns or neighborhoods outside of urban areas _____

10. The middle of the day _____

11. To make a change in appearance or behavior

_____

**Write your own sentences using three of the words from
either the Practice activity or the activity above.**

12. _____

_____

_____

13. _____

_____

14. _____

_____

Word Analysis • *Skills Practice*

Art of the Ancients

In 1940, a teenager wriggled into a narrow hole in the hills of France. Suddenly, he tumbled down some rocks. He found himself inside a cave! He called to his three friends to follow him. When the boys lifted their lanterns, they discovered an amazing sight. The walls were decorated with large paintings of colorful animals. The boys had discovered the art of an ancient community.

Their discovery created a sensation. Soon people were coming from far and wide to see the art. It was determined that the paintings were about 17,000 years old. The cave entrance was enlarged. Tourists could enter more easily. The floors were lowered. Tourists could walk without ducking their heads. By the 1950s, almost 1,200 people a day were flocking to the cave.

Why were so many people fascinated by the cave paintings? For one thing, the paintings are colorful and full of life. Hundreds of animals are portrayed on the cave walls. There are also mysterious signs and symbols on the walls. Some scientists believe that the symbols are an early form of writing.

Perhaps the biggest mystery of all is why the cave art was created. There are many theories. Some think that the cave art was created for tribal ceremonies. Perhaps they marked the end of childhood and the beginning of adulthood. Scientists have found some evidence to support this theory. They have discovered the footprints of children in some of the caves.

Others think the cave art was a way to store information that helped people survive. Perhaps the art showed where to hunt for animals during different seasons. Perhaps the mysterious signs were part of a hunting map or calendar.

Another theory is that the cave art recorded tribal myths and history. Before printing was invented, people had to memorize these stories. The images in the caves might have helped them remember. Perhaps different images illustrated different tales.

We may never know exactly why the cave art was created. Scientists continue to hunt for clues. Meanwhile, we can enjoy what we see—the lively animals, the mysterious signs, and the skill of the ancient artists.

In 1940, when the boys discovered the cave, the paintings were well preserved. The community that once inhabited it had disappeared. No humans had been there for almost 17,000 years. But by 1963, tourists had brought dangerous changes to the cave. They tracked in pollen and algae. The body heat doubled the temperature in the cave. Their breath contained moisture that built up on the walls.

Soon the paintings began to disappear. In order to save the paintings, the French government made a difficult choice. They closed the cave to tourists. Now only five people a day can enter the cave. They can only stay for thirty-five minutes.

Tourists still wanted to see the beautiful artwork from the ancient community though. So a replica of the cave was built. Tourists can explore it as if they were going through the real cave. Meanwhile, the original artwork is protected. Researchers hope this will help preserve the art for many generations to come.

Fluency • *Skills Practice*

Words with the Same Base

FOCUS
- **Words with the same base** belong to a family of words. The base word itself does not have any prefixes, suffixes, or inflectional endings added to it. Therefore, a base word can stand alone. When you add a prefix or suffix (or both) to the base word, the word's meaning changes. Sometimes, the part of speech changes as well. Example: **Base word** → fortune ("to have great luck")
  Words with the same base as *fortune* →
  <u>mis</u>fortune, fortun<u>ate</u>, <u>un</u>fortunate<u>ly</u>

PRACTICE Circle the words that belong to the same base word family in each row. Then write the base word on the line.

1. abrupt   abundantly   abundance   _____

2. uncooperative   cooking   cooperation   _____

3. disassociated   association   negotiate   _____

4. inobservant   obviously   observations   _____

5. jacket   enact   active   _____

6. reconnect   disconnected   collection   _____

APPLY Read each sentence. Change the underlined base word to a word from the word box that makes more sense in the sentence. Write the new word on the line.

recharge	powerful	endangered	proclaimed
greedy	description	resourceful	instructor
irresponsible	criminal	migration	appointment

7. The <u>crime</u> was caught trying to steal from the store. _____

8. Omar wrote a <u>describe</u> of his most recent trip to the art museum.
_____

9. Throughout time, many civilizations have learned to be <u>resource</u>.
_____

10. Leigh was punished for acting in a very <u>responsible</u> manner.
_____

11. "We need to find a new goalkeeper!" Jackson <u>claim</u>.
_____

12. Before she left home, Tamera made sure to <u>charge</u> her cell phone.
_____

13. Mom scheduled my next dentist <u>appoint</u> for next Tuesday.
_____

14. Our golf <u>instruct</u> taught us how to putt the golf ball.
_____

15. A <u>power</u> thunderstorm threatened the homes along the coast.
_____

16. Scientists carefully study the yearly <u>migrate</u> of birds.
_____

17. Humpback whales and killer whales are both <u>danger</u> species.
_____

18. I am not fond of people who are <u>greed</u>. _____

Word Analysis • *Skills Practice*

Shades of Meaning

> **FOCUS** • Words with **shades of meaning** have nearly the same definitions. However, there are slight differences in their meanings. In a set of similar words, think about which word has the strongest or most powerful shade of meaning.
> Example: *good → great → wonderful*
> *Great* is slightly better than *good*. *Wonderful* is slightly better than *great*.

PRACTICE Read each set of words. Rank the words according to their shades of meaning. The weakest or least powerful word should come first. The second weakest or least powerful word should come second. The strongest or most powerful word should come third. Write the words in their correct order on the line below each set of words.

1. hyper, awake, active

_____

2. pour, drip, flow

_____

3. demand, suggest, hint

_____

4. hot, mild, scorching

_____

APPLY Read each pair of words. Think about the relationship of the first word to the second word. Then look at the words listed below. Write the word that has the strongest/most powerful or weakest/least powerful shade of meaning on the line.

5. aged → old → _____
   different   ancient   elder

6. bother → frustrate → _____
   abrupt   hopeful   enrage

7. breezy → windy → _____
   calm   gusty   foggy

8. instruct → direct → _____
   command   answer   share

9. muffled → quiet → _____
   brave   tough   silent

10. hill → bluff → _____
    waterfall   valley   mountain

11. pretty → beautiful → _____
    plain   gorgeous   kind

12. grouch → complain → _____
    protest   assist   hurry

Planning a Community

A community is a place in which you live, work, and play. It is made up of people and resources. Today we live in many kinds of communities. There are small towns and large cities. They are found in mountains or plains and along rivers.

Many early communities were located near water. Living near water had many benefits. Poor roads made travel by land tough and slow. It was easier for people to move goods by boat. Communities built near rivers or the ocean grew quickly.

When the United States was a new country, the leaders knew they needed a capital city. After much dispute, the nation's leaders finally agreed to build a new city on the Potomac River. George Washington was asked to pick the actual site. He chose an area with thick forests and farmland, now called the District of Columbia.

The new capital would be unlike earlier cities that had grown with little thought about design and layout. This community was designed well before any construction began. Washington hired his friend Pierre Charles L'Enfant, a French engineer, to draw up plans.

In 1776, L'Enfant left his home in France. He made the long trip to the colonies. He fought against English rule, then he stayed in the new nation after the war. L'Enfant liked life in the United States. He believed the new country would become great.

Because of this, L'Enfant wanted the capital to be the greatest city in the world. He studied the land. He wanted to put the important buildings in the best places.

He wanted the streets to be wide and easy to navigate. For L'Enfant, the open spaces were as important as the roads and buildings. In these spaces, he put fountains and monuments. He also kept the height of all buildings at no more than 160 feet. This let light and air reach the streets.

Washington liked the plans. But other men had their own ideas. L'Enfant did not want their advice. One wealthy local man was building his house where L'Enfant wanted to place a street. L'Enfant had the house torn down! After many more clashes like this, Washington had to fire L'Enfant. His plans were still used, but by men more willing to compromise.

The struggles to build the new community did not end once the plan was done. Because building costs were high, work took place slowly. The president's house was begun in 1792. When John Adams became the second president in 1797, it was still not finished. Work on the Capitol Building began in 1793. The Senate first met there in 1800. Only one wing of the building had been built.

It took many years before the capital city would look as L'Enfant had planned. But his design has stood the test of time. It has lasted for more than two hundred years with very few major changes. Low buildings still allow light to reach the streets. Trees line wide avenues. Open spaces are abundant.

L'Enfant's vision of an American community lives on today in Washington, D.C.

Fluency • *Skills Practice*

Prefixes and Suffixes

> **FOCUS** A **prefix** is a word part added to the beginning of a base word or root. A **suffix** is a word part added to the end of a base word or root.
>
> - Examine the following prefixes and their meanings:
>   **oct-** ("eight") <u>oct</u>opus
>   **cent-** ("one hundred") <u>cent</u>ipede
>   **semi-** ("half") <u>semi</u>tropical
>   **para-** ("beside") <u>para</u>graph
> - Examine the following suffixes and their meanings:
>   **-dom** ("state or quality of") king<u>dom</u>
>   **-ship** ("state or quality of") owner<u>ship</u>
>   **-ent** ("inclined to") persist<u>ent</u>
>   **-ous** ("full of") myster<u>ous</u>

PRACTICE Read each word below. Circle the prefix or suffix found in the words.

1. hazardous

2. authorship

3. centimeter

4. deterrent

5. semiannual

6. magnified

7. octave

8. freedom

APPLY Match each word below with its meaning.

9. parallel   **a.** full of the desire to learn new things

10. wisdom   **b.** existing next to

11. curious   **c.** a person between the ages of 80 and 89

12. octogenarian   **d.** inclined to be neglectful

13. centurion   **e.** the quality of being wise

14. negligent   **f.** partly professional

15. companionship   **g.** an ancient Roman officer who commanded 100 men

16. semiprofessional   **h.** the quality of having a companion, or friend

Write two sentences using words from either the Practice activity or the activity above.

17. _____

_____

18. _____

_____

Prefixes and Suffixes

FOCUS A **prefix** is a word part added to the beginning of a base word or root. A **suffix** is a word part added to the end of a base word or root.

- Examine the following prefixes and their meanings:

  post- ("after") <u>post</u>graduate

  micro- ("small, short") <u>micro</u>phone

  ir- ("not") <u>ir</u>regular

  il- ("not") <u>il</u>legal

- Examine the following suffixes and their meanings:

  -ance/-ence ("state or quality of") viol<u>ence</u>

  -ize ("to make") energ<u>ize</u>

  -ist ("one who practices") biolog<u>ist</u>

  -ish ("relating to") self<u>ish</u>

PRACTICE Read each definition. Find the word from the word box that matches each definition and write it on the line.

reluctance	English	finalize	postmodern

1. The period *after* the modern time or era began _____

2. *Related to* England _____

3. *The state of* being reluctant _____

4. *To make* something final _____

APPLY Complete each sentence by writing a word from the word box on the line. Use the definition of the prefix or suffix in parentheses to help you determine the answer.

sluggish	postproduction	capitalize	irresistible	lyricist
microphone	publicize	importance	dependence	extradite

5. Bree could not emphasize enough the _____ of doing research on the topic. ("*the quality of* being important")

6. The lead singer is using a _____ so the audience can hear her. ("a device used to transmit sound or to make it louder")

7. We noticed that the writer forgot to _____ the first word in the sentence. ("*to make* a capital letter")

8. The film crew was in _____. ("the period *after* a movie or show has been filmed")

9. The company plans to _____ its most recent advertising campaign. ("*to make* something publicly known)

10. In his rock band, Miguel is the drummer and _____. ("*one who practices* writing music lyrics")

11. The judge is trying to determine whether to _____ the criminal. ("to send a criminal *outside* of, or away from, the current state or country for trial")

12. Jordan is feeling tired and _____ today. ("*related to* being inactive or unmotivated")

13. Petting the puppies was _____ for the children. ("not capable of being resisted")

14. A baby's _____ on his or her parent or caretaker is very important. ("*the state of* being dependent")

Word Analysis • *Skills Practice*

Fluency Checklist

As you read the following poem, be sure to keep these things in mind to help you read with the appropriate rate, accuracy, and expression.

As you read, make sure you

☐ pause longer at a period or other ending punctuation.

☐ raise your voice at a question mark.

☐ use expression when you come to an exclamation point.

☐ pause at commas but not as long as you would at a period.

☐ think of the character and how he or she might say his or her words whenever you come to quotation marks.

☐ remember not to read so fast that someone listening could not hear the individual words or make sense of what is being read.

☐ stop and reread something that does not make sense.

Our Story

Our history is like a story.
Once upon a time,
millions of buffalo
thundered across the plains.
Native Americans lived
in the tall, waving grasses;
in the forests and mountains.

But once upon a time,
many lost their sacred lands,
their freedom, and their lives.
The buffalo were hunted
until they almost vanished.
Whole forests
were cut for lumber.

Our history is like a story.
We cannot change the past
but we can write
a better future.

The Great Migration

Big changes often start with someone's dreams. The Great Migration was a big change that made a huge impact on the United States. Over nearly 70 years, nearly six million African Americans moved. Whole communities traveled from the South to northern cities. They dreamt of a better life. Their move changed our country.

Many people with different ideas met for the first time. In these new communities, fresh art and musical styles developed. Our country would not be the same without the many people who left home to follow their dreams.

In the 1900s, the South was the location of most African American communities. But it was not an easy place for them to be. There was a lot of tension among social classes. African Americans in the South were not treated the same as other people.

Some people wanted to make sure that this treatment stayed unequal. Southern governments set up laws to limit rights. These laws were unjust. Farms were also beginning to fail. The workers in the South depended on farms. Without them, they had no money.

It is no wonder so many African Americans wanted to leave. But the choice to leave your community is not always easy. The South is home to a rich heritage. This heritage includes food, music, language, and customs. These things are often the first things we think of when we think of home.

Migrating African Americans brought some of the best parts of the South with them. They moved to the North with great hope. They wanted more work, more money, and better places to live. They hoped for a better place in society. They believed that in the North, they would be treated fairly. They wanted equal justice.

And soon, the migrating African Americans began to find what they were looking for. They settled in communities that appealed to different talents. Many musicians went to Chicago. Chicago became known for its blues and jazz. Writers and artists found a strong community in Harlem, a part of New York City. Workers needing jobs turned to the industry of Detroit. Other cities developed thriving communities as well.

News of these new communities of African Americans spread back to the South. More and more people began to migrate north. It is easy to see the importance of the Great Migration. Those who moved north increased diversity in communities all over the country.

The success of these communities helped others stand up for their rights. Together, people began to push for civil rights.

The Great Migration spread dreams and ideas across the United States. It helped all people who were seeking a better life. African Americans faced many challenges. Yet they overcame them and set an example for others. They held on to their hopes and dreams. They carried them to their new communities, and they grew.

We can thank the people of the Great Migration for showing us that everyone should have an equal chance.

Clothes for the Community

Clara stared into her closet. The gray day and the drumming of the rain against her window made her sluggish. With a sigh she selected something to wear.

As Clara rummaged through her clothes, she came to a sudden stop. She stepped back to survey her closet with a more critical eye and a smile spread across her face. Now filled with energy, Clara hurriedly got dressed and bounded down the stairs.

"Good morning, Clara," Mom greeted her. "Have you decided on a community service project for school yet?" she asked.

Clara grinned broadly, "Mom, I have the best idea ever!"

Mom smiled at Clara's enthusiasm. "Well, let's hear it!" she urged.

"You know that I have had a hard time deciding what to do," began Clara. "Well, I was just trying to find something to wear. I was staring at my closet, and I realized I have clothes that I never wear. Why not put them to good use? So, I decided that I want to organize a community clothing drive. Would you and Dad participate?"

"Of course," said Mom, "what do you have in mind?"

"We can go through our closets," said Clara. "We can donate to charity anything that is in good shape that we are not using."

Clara and Mom peered into the downstairs closet.

"Look at all this stuff!" said Clara.

They continued to explore closets throughout the house.

"Wow, this makes me realize how much I take for granted," said Clara.

"How so?" asked Mom.

"I always think I need more outfits to wear, but that is not true," said Clara. "Looking at all this stuff makes me realize how lucky I am. Many people in our community do not have basic necessities. It is my duty to share with them."

"That is a great attitude to have," said Mom.

"What if we include the whole neighborhood?" asked Clara. "That way we could get everyone involved in doing their duty."

"Sounds great," said Mom. "We can have people drop their donations here. We will plan it for a weekend so more people will be available."

"Maybe we can get the whole community together," Clara hoped.

They began sorting the items from the closets.

"I cannot wait for Dad to get home," said Clara. "He will be excited about this. I never knew how much fun it could be to help out our community," she continued. "I want to think of more ways to help others."

"Count me in!" said Mom.

Fluency • *Skills Practice*

Compound Words, Antonyms and Synonyms

FOCUS • A **compound word** is one word that has two smaller words in it. Sometimes a compound word has the same meaning as the two words in it. Sometimes it has a new meaning.

shoe + lace = shoelace	**"a *lace* that is used to tie a *shoe*"**
air + line = airline	**"air transportation company"** (not "a *line* in the *air*")

An open compound is two separate words that are read together and have a single meaning.

vice president	**"a person who is second in command at a company"**

PRACTICE A Circle the compound word in each sentence. Write a definition for each word, using a dictionary as necessary if you need help.

1. Mom placed a scented candle in the candlestick.

_____

2. Our babysitter watched us for several hours after school.

_____

3. Jenessa mailed a letter at the post office.

_____

4. The birds begin chirping at the first sign of daylight.

_____

• **Antonyms** are words that have opposite meanings.
Polite and *rude* are antonyms.

• **Synonyms** are words with the same or nearly the same meanings.
Polite and *courteous* are synonyms.

A dictionary or thesaurus can help you find synonyms and antonyms.

PRACTICE B Read the following sentences. Then answer the questions below.

Miranda was *bothered* by the very loud music coming from her brother's room.

5. Look in a thesaurus or dictionary.
Find two synonyms for the word *bothered*. _____ _____

6. Find an antonym for the word *bothered*. _____

7. If words are synonyms, they should each have a similar meaning within a sentence. Could your synonyms replace *bothered* in the sentence? _____

The jury members will *examine* the evidence to determine whether the defendant is *guilty* or *innocent*.

8. Look up *examine* in a thesaurus.
What are two synonyms for *examine*? _____ _____

9. What is an antonym for *examine*? _____

10. Which two words in the sentence are antonyms?

_____ _____

　　　　　　　　　　Word Analysis • *Skills Practice*

Shades of Meaning, Regular and Irregular Plurals

> **FOCUS**
> - Words with different **shades of meaning** have nearly the same definitions. However, there are slight differences in their meanings. In a set of similar words, think about which word has the strongest or most powerful shade of meaning.
>
>   Example: **big → large → enormous**
>
>   *Large* is of greater size than *big*. *Enormous* is of greater size than *large*.

PRACTICE A **Read the following sentences. Think about the meanings of the underlined words. Place these words in order according to their shades of meaning. Start with the least powerful word, and end with the most powerful word.**

1. Anya became <u>overjoyed</u> upon receiving the news that her friend planned to visit from Russia.
Devon was <u>happy</u> to represent his school at the spelling bee.
Rachel is <u>content</u> reading a book on a rainy Saturday afternoon.

_____ _____ _____

Read each pair of words. Complete each series of words by writing a word that has the strongest or most powerful shade of meaning.

bizarre	filthy	sobbing

2. crying → weeping → _____

3. unusual → strange → _____

4. dirty → soiled → _____

FOCUS

- To make many nouns plural, add the ending -s, -es, -ies, or -ves. These types of plurals are called regular plurals, because they follow certain rules. For example:

windo**w**	+	**s**	=	windo**ws**		
bea**ch**	+	**es**	=	bea**ches**		
territor**y**	–	**y**	+	**ies**	=	territor**ies**
thie**f**	–	**f**	+	**ves**	=	thie**ves**

- Some plural nouns do not follow the regular pattern. These are called **irregular plurals**.

Some words, such as **salmon** and **moose**, have the same singular and plural forms.

Other words, such as **woman**, change spellings in the plural form. For example, **woman** becomes **women** in the plural form.

PRACTICE B Write the regular plural noun form of each given word.

5. paintbrush _____

6. wolf _____

7. dream _____

8. factory _____

Write the irregular plural noun form for each given description.

9. one fish several _____

10. one tooth thirty-two _____

11. one deer a herd of _____

12. one child four _____

Singers of History

A man plucks the strings of his instrument and sings out proudly. He is sitting in the town square. A crowd is gathering around him, anxious for him to begin. Many people in his West African village have come to listen. They know he may sing for days, and they are eager to hear him. He is singing the history of their clan.

This man is a West African griot (GREE-oh). Griots are historians and musicians combined. The griots' job is to sing the history of a clan. They pass on stories and traditions. Those who hear them feel pride. They feel proud of their past and they feel proud of their clan.

It is said when a griot dies, a library has disappeared. Like the books in a library, griots hold much wisdom. Unlike books in a library, their wisdom is not written down. It is memorized and sung in songs. The job of a griot is passed from parent to child. Griot parents teach their songs to a son or daughter.

Griots have long been part of West African culture. Starting in the twelfth century, griots worked in the castles of kings. Their songs praised the king and his family. They told great tales of the kingdom's history. Since griots knew so much, they were said to be wise. They used what they knew to help solve the king's problems.

The songs griots sing are about big events in the clan's history. They mention births and deaths of well-known members. They sing of the ancestors of the clan. They tell of marriages, of hunts that took place, and of wars. It takes years of training to become a griot. When they are young, some modern griots live for several years with a wise man for training. They may work in the fields when they are not studying.

Young griots learn hundreds of songs. They learn how to sing and play the drums. They may learn to play the balaphone. The balaphone has bars that are struck like a xylophone. It is most common in the country of Guinea. Another instrument, the kora, has 21 strings and sounds like a harp. It is most popular in the country of Gambia.

When they become adults, young griots may take over their parents' jobs as griots. They train for years to learn their art. Some play and sing in restaurants and on the beach. They share their cultural traditions with tourists. Some modern griots teach at griot schools. They help others learn to be griots.

Griots are part of an ancient tradition. But griots are still valued in modern times. A few work in the homes of the rich. Most work for themselves. Some are even pop stars. But griots still sing the histories of tribes and families. They take part in namings, weddings, and other big events. They travel from town to town, telling stories. Griots help West Africans feel proud of their past. Griots take history and turn it into a performance.

Contractions, Possessives, Irregular Verbs, and Abstract Nouns

> **Focus**
> - A **contraction** is formed from two words. Some letters are left out when the words are combined. An apostrophe (') marks the spot where the letters were dropped.
>   *he's* → *he + is*   *we'll* → *we + will*
> - A **possessive noun** shows who or what owns or possesses something. Consider the following question: "Whose sweater is this?" Answer: "This sweater belongs to Sergio. It is *Sergio's* sweater." *Sergio's* is the possessive noun.
>   **the *writer's* notebook**   **the *athletes'* uniforms**

PRACTICE A Read each sentence below. Circle the two pairs of words in each sentence that can be made into contractions. Write the contractions on the line.

1. Erin should have left for school earlier, but she had forgotten to set her alarm.

_____

2. We are planning to leave, but there is a problem with our car.

_____

Read each sentence below. Write the possessive form of the underlined word.

3. We located the <u>hospital</u> entrance after walking around the building.

_____

4. The <u>judges</u> robes are long and black. _____

Focus • **Irregular verbs** are verbs that do not follow a normal pattern. With **regular verbs**, the *-ed* ending is added to make the past tense.

Examples: *jump* (present), *jumped* (past)

Irregular verbs take on different forms in the past tense. They do not include the *-ed* ending.

Examples: *make* (present), *made* (past)
think (present), *thought* (past)

• **Abstract nouns** name feelings or ideas. You cannot see, hear, smell, taste, or touch them. For example, *sorrow* and *knowledge* are abstract nouns. However, words such as *brother* and *carrot* are not abstract nouns, because they can be observed through the senses.

PRACTICE B Match each present-tense irregular verb with its past-tense form.

5. sleep   a. sent

6. lose   b. left

7. leave   c. slept

8. send   d. lost

Read each sentence below. Circle the abstract noun in each sentence. Underline any nouns that are not abstract.

9. I was thankful for the man's generosity.

10. My sister has had much success making and selling her artwork.

11. Lily experienced jealousy when her friend got a new bike.

12. The book focused on the romance of a young man and woman.

Word Analysis • *Skills Practice*

Homophones, Homographs, and Multiple-Meaning Words

> **FOCUS**   **Homophones** are words that sound alike but have different spellings and different meanings. Think about the meaning of the word when spelling a homophone.
>
> Example: **Weather** and **whether** are homophones.
>
> The words sound like: (we' thər)
>
> But they have different meanings:
>
> *weather* "the conditions of the atmosphere at any given time"
>
> *whether* "suggesting a choice or possibility"

PRACTICE A   Answer the questions below.

1. What is the meaning of the underlined word in the sentence below?

After the beloved man passed away, many people were in <u>mourning</u> at his funeral.

_____

2. What is the meaning of the underlined word in the sentence below?

In the <u>morning</u>, Remi wakes up and eats breakfast with her family.

_____

3. Are *mourning* and *morning* homophones? Why or why not?

_____

4. Use *mourning* or *morning* to correctly complete this sentence:

My friend and I went jogging earlier this _____.

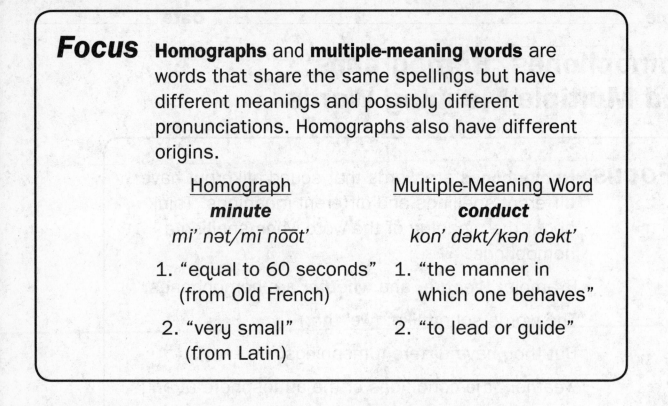

FOCUS Homographs and multiple-meaning words are words that share the same spellings but have different meanings and possibly different pronunciations. Homographs also have different origins.

Homograph	Multiple-Meaning Word
minute	*conduct*
mi' nət/mī nōōt'	kon' dəkt/kən dəkt'
1. "equal to 60 seconds" (from Old French)	1. "the manner in which one behaves"
2. "very small" (from Latin)	2. "to lead or guide"

PRACTICE B Answer the questions below. Use a dictionary to determine the word meanings and origins.

5. Sentence 1: Jada made sure the <u>content</u> in her paper was interesting.

Sentence 2: I am quite <u>content</u> reading a book on the beach.

What is the meaning and origin of *content* in Sentence 2?

_____

6. Use one of the meanings of the word *content* in a sentence of your own.

_____

_____

7. The ocean <u>current</u> is strong today, so people should not go surfing.

What is the definition of the multiple-meaning word *current*, as it is used in the sentence above?

_____

8. What is another definition for the word *current*?

_____

Word Analysis • *Skills Practice*

Journey into Jazz

As night falls in New Orleans, musicians gather on a stage. They begin to tune their instruments. Listeners wait eagerly. A rich melody pours into the evening. Then, above its steady beat, a solo begins to soar. The musician repeats the melody, then begins to change it and shape it in a different way. One by one, the players pass the melody and invent new ways for it to flow. This magical music is jazz. It has been flowing and changing for over a century. But its roots go back much further than that.

Jazz music got its start in New Orleans. It joined the feelings of blues with the off-beat tempo of ragtime. It was not predictable. It took the form of a song and let soloists play with it. The soloists' play was called improvisation. They made up music on the spur of the moment. Jazz musicians varied the tune to put their personal stamp on it. And as people migrated north from New Orleans, jazz moved with them.

By the 1920s, America was ready for the newness of jazz. It was around this time that America entered a prosperous era. The economy was booming. People had money to spend. They bought new inventions such as radios and record players. They listened joyfully to high-spirited jazz. It filled the airwaves and spread into homes and dance halls.

In the 1930s, as jazz grew more popular, large groups of jazz musicians began to play together. Out of these big bands, an exciting new style of jazz began. The big band sound, known as swing, swept the country. Swing music took improvisation to a new level. Its fast pace was a great influence on dancing. Dancing became freer, livelier, and more original. Dance halls were the place to be, and big band music helped lift the spirits of the nation.

In the 1940s, jazz musicians continued to develop their art. New forms, such as bebop, appeared. Bebop included even more complex rhythms and tunes. Bebop solos contained more twists and turns than a mountain stream. Bebop was played at a very fast tempo as well. Each new form of jazz has added to its richness.

By the 1950s, Americans found new forms of entertainment. They began to watch television. Teenagers were caught up in rock music. The jazz dance halls that were once crowded had to close. Smaller bands replaced the big bands of the past. And jazz changed again and survived.

True to its beginnings, jazz continues to change over the years. It has been influenced by music from other cultures. It has also been adapted and used in other music forms. Rock music usually has a steady beat. But some rock musicians grew bored with its repetition. They introduced jazz phrasing and solos over the steady beat.

Jazz was created by joining the best of many types of music. It continues to draw in elements of music from around the world. In turn, other cultures have borrowed from jazz to create new music. Jazz will continue to grow and change as new talent and ideas flow into the music.

Inflectional Endings, Regular and Irregular Comparative and Superlatives

Focus • The **inflectional ending -ed** shows that the action has happened in the past. The **inflectional ending -ing** shows that the action is happening now or always happens.

Examples: **admit → admitted score → scored**
apply → applied

plan → planning prove → proving
marry → marrying

PRACTICE A Read each sentence. Change the verb to the proper tense using an inflectional ending.

1. Our teacher <u>supply</u> us with construction paper and markers.
   _____

2. I will be <u>demonstrate</u> how to make a necklace. _____

3. Dexter is <u>carry</u> bags of groceries. _____

4. Evangelina <u>state</u>, "Please cross the street at the crosswalk."
   _____

5. We ignored the rules and <u>regret</u> our poor decision. _____

6. After the heavy rainfall, water began <u>drip</u> from the spouts.
   _____

7. The company's manager is <u>suggest</u> they they develop a new product. _____

Focus

- **Comparatives** compare two nouns or verbs. **Superlatives** compare three or more nouns or verbs. To make an adjective or adverb a comparative, add *er* for shorter words. Use the word *more* before some longer words.

  To make an adjective or adverb a superlative, add *-est* for shorter words. Use the word *most* before some longer adjectives and adverbs.

  Examples: **fast** → **faster** → **fastest**

  quietly → **more quietly** → **most quietly**

- Some **comparatives** and **superlatives** are irregular. This means they do not follow the normal rules.

  little → *less* → *least*

PRACTICE B Circle the correct regular comparative or superlative in each sentence.

8. The (tougher/toughest) competition will be at the end of the season.

9. Tara walked (more hurriedly/most hurriedly) than her Aunt Dawn.

Choose an irregular comparative or superlative from the box to complete each sentence.

worst	farthest	worse

10. The _____ snowstorm I've seen happened last winter.

11. My dad had a bad cold, but mine was even _____.

12. Damon's last hike was the _____ he had ever gone.

Word Analysis • *Skills Practice*

Content Words, Shades of Meaning, and Words with the Same Base

> **FOCUS**
> - **Content words** are specific to a topic or a subject area. Think about words that are related to the topic of government. For example, the word *legislature* means "elected officials who have the power to create or change laws."
> - Words with **shades of meaning** have nearly the same definitions. However, there are slight differences in the words' meanings.
>
>   Example: *cool → cold → freezing*

PRACTICE A Circle two content words in each set of words that are related to the topic of government. Write a definition for one of the two words.

1. damage   liberty   citizenship   temperature

   _____

2. habitat   election   phrase   taxation

   _____

Read the pair of words below and think about the relationship between them. Use a thesaurus to locate a third word that has a stronger shade of meaning. Write the word on the line.

3. amusing, funny, _____

4. sip, drink, _____

Focus • **Words with the same base** belong to a family of words. The base word itself does not have any prefixes, suffixes, or inflectional endings added to it. Therefore, a base word can stand alone. When you add a prefix or suffix (or both) to the base word, the word's meaning changes. Sometimes, the part of speech changes as well.

Example: **Base word** → **adjust** ("to change something in order to make it better")

Words with the same base as adjust →
<u>re</u>adjust, adjust<u>ment</u>, adjust<u>ing</u>

PRACTICE B Read each sentence below. Circle the word that can replace the underlined word in the sentence.

5. The elections were held in an <u>fair</u> manner.

unfair   fairness   fairly

6. Our toaster <u>mystery</u> disappeared from the kitchen.

mysterious   mysteriousness   mysteriously

7. He was rewarded for his good <u>behave</u>.

misbehave   behavior   behaved

8. The president <u>claim</u>, "We must find a solution to this problem!"

proclaimed   disclaim   claiming

9. If someone commits an <u>legal</u> act, he or she is tried in the court of law.

illegal   legality   legalize

10. When traveling overseas, it is necessary to have proper <u>identify</u>.

unidentified   identification   identified

Fluency Checklist

As you read the following poem, be sure to keep these things in mind to help you read with the appropriate rate, accuracy, and expression.

As you read, make sure you

☐ pause longer at a period or other ending punctuation.

☐ raise your voice at a question mark.

☐ use expression when you come to an exclamation point.

☐ pause at commas but not as long as you would at a period.

☐ think of the character and how he or she might say his or her words whenever you come to quotation marks.

☐ remember not to read so fast that someone listening could not hear the individual words or make sense of what is being read.

☐ stop and reread something that does not make sense.

The Play

Today's the day! I'm going to act
with all my classmates in the play.
I practiced every afternoon
to be ready for this day.

When they raise the curtain high,
it's time for me to play my part.
I take a breath and step on stage
to say the lines I know by heart.

I see the set, I see the lights,
I see the faces in the crowd.
But I am brave. I'm not afraid.
Today my voice is clear and loud.

When I act, I make believe.
In my costume, I pretend
to be a character onstage.
I wish the play would never end.

But when the curtain falls, I know
my make believe is done for now.
All the people clap their hands.
It's time to smile and take a bow.

Suffixes *-y, -ly, -ful, -less, -ion/-tion/-sion,* and *-al,* and Latin Suffixes *-ment, -ive, -ity* and *-able*

FOCUS • A **suffix** is a word part added to the end of a base word or root that changes its meaning. Some common suffixes include the following:

-y ("full of")

-ly ("to do something in a certain way")

-ion/-tion/-sion ("state of being")

-less ("without" or "lacking")

-ful ("full of")

-al ("relating to")

PRACTICE A Write words from the word box to complete each sentence below. Each sentence will contain two words.

appreciation	electrical	homeless	terribly
shady	meaningful	approval	powerful

1. We wanted to do something _____ for the people at the _____ shelter.

2. Although our presentation had gone _____ wrong, we had _____ for our classmates' attention.

3. With their teacher's _____, the class read under a _____ tree on the warm, sunny day.

4. Last night, one _____ gust of wind knocked out our _____ system and left us in the dark.

FOCUS

• A **Latin suffix** is a word part derived from ancient Latin and can be added to the end of a base word or root. Latin suffixes can change the meaning, part of speech, and spelling of base words. Some common Latin suffixes include the following:

-ment ("action" or "process")　　**-ity** ("state of being")

-ive ("inclined to")　　**-able** ("can be")

PRACTICE B Correctly add the Latin suffixes *-ment*, *-ive*, *-ity*, or *-able* to each base word in the box to complete the sentence.

5. | humid + *-ity* |　The _____ of the jungle made everything feel damp and sticky.

6. | avoid + *-able* |　The accident would have been _____ if everyone had been watching where they were going.

7. | assign + *-ment* |　Rikki's homework _____ was to research the history of modern art.

8. | expense + *-ive* |　The jewelry store kept the most _____ items locked safely in a vault.

9. | judge + *-ment* |　In my _____, homemade pasta dishes are better than those you find in restaurants.

10. | disrupt + *-ive* |　The protestors were so _____ that the company agreed to stop using the chemicals in their products.

Multiple-Meaning Words; Suffixes -ness and -er, Content Words; Words with the Same Base; Greek and Latin Roots

> **FOCUS**
> - **Multiple-meaning words** are words that share the same spellings and origins, but have different meanings and possibly different pronunciations.
>
> - The suffix **-ness** means "state or quality of" and the suffix **-er** means "one who."
>
> - **Content words** are specific to a topic or a subject area. Think about words that are related to the topic of weather. For example, the word **wind chill** means "a cooling effect caused by the wind, which makes the air temperature feel colder than it really is."

PRACTICE A Read the sentence below. Write the underlined words' definitions based on how they are used, using a dictionary as necessary. Then define the word with the suffix -er using your knowledge of the suffix.

The reporter wrote a <u>column</u> about the company's decision to <u>fire</u> two workers.

1. _____

2. _____

3. _____

Circle the weather-related content word in each set of words.

4. capital   poisonous   occupation   monsoon

5. octagon   atmosphere   independent   ancestor

• **Words with the same base** belong to a family of words.

Example: **Base word** → *consider*

Words with the same base → *<u>re</u>consider,*
consider<u>ate</u>, consider<u>ing</u>

• **Greek** and **Latin roots** are word parts that have certain meanings. Some common roots include the following:

ast means "star." **graph** means "write."

log means "word." **scop** means "see."

grat means "pleasing."

mar means "sea."

miss means "send." **port** means "carry."

PRACTICE B Circle the words from the same base word family in each row, and then write the base word on the line.

6. substandard   standardize   statuette   _____

7. interruption   intensive   interrupted   _____

Think about the Greek or Latin root in each word below. Match each word with its definition.

8. marine

a. to tell people you are happy for them

9. autograph

b. a star-shaped symbol

10. congratulate

c. to carry something from one place to another

11. microscope

d. relating to the sea

12. transport

e. a special job a person is sent to finish

13. mission

f. a person's handwritten name

14. monologue

g. a speech in a play that is spoken by one person

15. asterisk

h. a tool used to look at small things

Word Analysis • *Skills Practice*

A Storyteller's Life

The students are excited, but they need to concentrate on their work. They talk in loud voices and wiggle in their chairs.

The teacher claps his hands to get their attention. "I promised you a reward if the class read a total of one hundred books this summer. Now someone is going to tell you a story."

A woman with curly red hair walks to the front of the room. "My name is Emily, and I'm a storyteller," she says. She looks at the children's eager faces. They are smiling, and some are whispering to each other. Emily begins her story and the children grow quiet and listen intently.

Emily has been telling stories all her life. She grew up in a family that loved to tell stories. They watched television and read books too. But they all told stories. Emily and her sister were encouraged to use their imaginations.

As a girl, Emily loved to read biographies. She read about Clara Barton and other famous women. Then she pretended to be them.

Emily's mother helped her pretend. She would say to her daughter, "Clara Barton, would you please set the table?"

If everyone was too busy to listen to a story, Emily would tell it to her cats or stuffed animals. If she was outside, she would tell a story to the trees, grass, and flowers. No one made her feel bad about her imagination.

When Emily grew up, she realized that being a storyteller could be her job. She learned from other storytellers. They taught her how to take apart a story and put it back together again.

Stories help us learn who we are and what we can do. People keep traditions alive by telling stories. Stories can teach us about our ancestors. They can help us understand our families and our communities.

Stories also show us how to behave. For example, your parents might tell you stories about how they got into trouble when they were children! You can find out what lessons they learned from their actions. Stories also help us learn about other times, places, and people.

Scarcely a day goes by without Emily telling a story. She spends much of her time visiting schools. She may share as many as twelve stories in one day with students. Emily encourages students to tell stories too. She travels around the country and the world telling her stories.

She observes that everyone has stories to tell. When people talk about things that happen to them, they are telling a story. And you can't tell a story wrong—even if it's different from the way others tell it.

Emily offers these tips about storytelling:

- Take your time.

- Look at your listeners.

- If you forget part of the story, make up something.

- If your mouth gets dry, don't clear your throat. Drink water slowly. Don't take big gulps.

- In most stories, things happen in threes. (Think of "Goldilocks and the Three Bears".) That will help you remember what comes next in the story.

- Start by telling a story to one person.

- Most of all—have fun!

Prefixes *re-, pre-, mis-, un-, con-, in-/im-, ex-, en-/em-, dis-, auto-,* and Number Prefixes

Focus • A **prefix** is a word part added to the beginning of a base word or root. Examine the following prefixes and their meanings:

re- ("again") *in-/im-* ("not")

pre- ("before") *ex-* ("out")

mis- ("wrongly") *en-/em-* ("in")

un- (the opposite of") *dis-* ("not")

con- ("with") *auto-* ("self")

Examples: **<u>re</u>start, <u>pre</u>wash, <u>mis</u>calculate, <u>un</u>afraid, <u>con</u>verge, <u>in</u>destructible, <u>ex</u>pire, <u>en</u>vision, <u>dis</u>honor, <u>auto</u>mobile**

PRACTICE A **Circle two words in each sentence that contain the prefixes described in the Focus box above.**

1. At my consultation, the doctor told me that I need to take some precautions to be healthier.

2. Aliyah was exempt from taking the pretest this week.

3. In her autobiography, the author mentions the injustices she dealt with as a young woman.

4. I am very disorganized, so I need to rethink my filing system.

5. Benson mishandled the situation by being unhelpful during a time when his friends needed assistance.

Focus • **Number prefixes** are prefixes that have to do with numbers. They tell you the amount of something. Examine the following prefixes and their meanings:

uni- ("one") **_unison_**   **tri-** ("three") **_triathlon_**

bi- ("two") **_biannual_**   **multi-** ("many") **_multimedia_**

PRACTICE B **Match each word that contains a number prefix with its meaning below.**

6. triplets   **a.** an animal with two feet

7. multipurpose   **b.** a shape that has three sides and angles

8. triangle   **c.** to do many things at the same time

9. unicycle   **d.** having many different purposes

10. bilingual   **e.** three babies born at the same time

11. biped   **f.** to bring together as one

12. multitask   **g.** a self-powered vehicle with one wheel

13. unify   **h.** able to speak two languages

Write a sentence using one of the words from the activity above.

14. _____

_____

Location Prefixes, Words with the Same Base, Shades of Meaning, and Prefixes and Suffixes

Focus • **Location prefixes** are prefixes that have to do with places or times. Examine the following prefixes and their meanings:

mid- ("middle") **trans-** ("across")

sub- ("under") **inter-** ("among" or "between")

• **Words with the same base** belong to a family of words.
Example: **Base word** → **forgive**

Words with the same base as forgive →
<u>un</u>forgive<u>able</u>, forgive<u>ness</u>, forgiv<u>ing</u>

PRACTICE A Match each word with its meaning below.

1. transistor   **a.** the middle of the week

2. midweek   **b.** an underground train system

3. interject   **c.** a device that controls electronic flow

4. subway   **d.** to insert a comment into a conversation

Circle the words from the same base word family in each row, and then write the base word on the line.

5. infection   reflecting   disinfect   _____

6. developed   delivery   undeliverable   _____

Focus • Words with differing **shades of meaning** have nearly the same definitions. However, there are slight differences in the words' meanings.

Example: *gully* → *ravine* → *canyon*

• **Prefixes** and **suffixes** are word parts added to base words and roots. Knowing the meanings of prefixes and suffixes can help clarify the meanings of unfamiliar words.

PRACTICE B Circle two words in each sentence that contain the prefixes and suffixes you have studied. Write a synonym with a different shade of meaning for each underlined word, using a thesaurus as necessary.

7. The semiprecious stone was made into a <u>glamorous</u> ring.

_____

8. The postgraduate was very efficient at completing <u>difficult</u> projects.

_____

9. Krista is a zoologist who <u>studies</u> creatures such as centipedes.

_____

10. The octogenarian had attained a great deal of <u>wisdom</u> over her long lifetime.

_____

11. We took an introductory course on how to <u>gain</u> leadership qualities.

_____

12. I felt foolish after someone <u>commented</u> on my performance.

Word Analysis • *Skills Practice*

Fluency Checklist

As you read the following poem, be sure to keep these things in mind to help you read with the appropriate rate, accuracy, and expression.

As you read, make sure you

☐ pause longer at a period or other ending punctuation.

☐ raise your voice at a question mark.

☐ use expression when you come to an exclamation point.

☐ pause at commas but not as long as you would at a period.

☐ think of the character and how he or she might say his or her words whenever you come to quotation marks.

☐ remember not to read so fast that someone listening could not hear the individual words or make sense of what is being read.

☐ stop and reread something that does not make sense.

The Big Bad Wolf Speaks

Believe me when I tell you
I am big, but I am not bad.
I am wild like the woods.
Didn't your mother warn you
about wild things
when she handed you the basket
for your grandmother?

Through the trees I can see
your red hood and cape.
I can hear leaves crunching
under your feet as you come closer.
I have not eaten in days.
I'm sorry, but I am hungry enough
to swallow someone whole.

Little Red Riding Hood,
the good part of me wishes
you would turn and go home.
Visit your grandmother another day.
Believe me when I tell you
I am big, but I am not bad.

Art for Our Ancestors

Joe Kingbird's mom said, "You'll have a wonderful time, Joe."

"But you and Dad aren't even coming," Joe whined.

"What kind of attitude is that?" his mom replied, smiling. "Your grandfather is really looking forward to it. Besides, we have to travel for work; we couldn't go with you anyway."

Joe was not happy about visiting his grandfather. Especially since his friends were all at the beach.

It was a long drive to Grandfather's house. When they finally pulled in, Grandfather was waiting for them. As Joe got out of the car, he was shocked to see his grandfather. He wasn't dressed in his usual khaki pants and polo shirt; today he wore something *much* different.

"Hello Joseph, we're going to a Powwow today!" his grandfather exclaimed. "That is why I am dressed this way." Joe did not know what a Powwow was, but if his grandfather wanted to go, it was probably boring and old-fashioned.

"Don't worry, I'll show you what it is," Grandfather said. "You should learn about your Native American heritage." They hopped in the car and headed out. By the time they arrived, it was already crowded.

"These people have come from all over the United States," Grandfather explained. "It's a way to honor our ancestors." As they approached a grassy area, Joe heard a deep drum.

"Can we watch the performance?" he asked.

"Yes," Grandfather said, "The singing has started already, so we should hurry."

Joe settled down on the grass to watch. To his surprise, Grandfather did not sit with him. Instead, he joined the line of singers. After waiting for his turn, he began to sing. His voice was clear and deep. After the song, Joe rushed to join Grandfather.

"I didn't know you could sing like that! It was beautiful!"

"Thank you," Grandfather said. "There are others with stronger voices. I just do it for enjoyment, and to honor our ancestors. Now, would you like to see the men's traditional dance?"

The two watched as men whirled and stomped to the rhythm. It was the most magnificent thing Joe had ever seen. When the dance ended, one of the dancers strolled over.

"Do you have time for me to show you a few steps?" the dancer asked.

"Sure!" Joe replied. The dancer went slowly, and Joe watched carefully so he could imitate the steps.

"Excellent, now you are ready," the dancer told Joe.

"Ready for what?" Joe asked.

"Ready to join us in the dance," the dancer answered. This made Joe nervous. He did not want to look silly next to the better dancers.

"The steps are symbolic," the dancer told him. "Visualize all those who came before you and think of a way to—"

"Honor our ancestors!" Joe finished.

"Exactly," said the dancer as the music began again. At first, Joe watched, but soon he whirled, twirled, and stomped with the rest. The drums excited him and made him proud.

"When is the next Powwow?" Joe asked as the music stopped.

"Soon, but what about the beach?" replied Grandfather.

"The beach can wait, but honoring our ancestors through song and dance can't!" Joe exclaimed.

Martha Graham and Modern Dance

Martha Graham is known as a pioneer of modern dance. She brought her ideas to life on the American stage. She experimented with movement. She used to dance to express her feelings. Her dances featured sharp, jagged motions. They surprised viewers expecting the flowing, smooth ballet dances of the time.

At age twenty-two, Graham joined a famous dance school. Dancers usually begin when they are many years younger. But Martha Graham was anything but the usual dancer. She spent seven years with that dance company. There, she learned both American and world dance. Then she went solo.

Graham moved to New York City, where she developed her own style. The way the body moves had always interested Graham. Her father was a doctor and had observed movement to diagnose disorders. As a young athlete, Graham became aware of her own motions and movements.

She began to choreograph, or create, her own dances, as well as teach dance to others. At the Eastman School of Music, Graham directed the entire dance program. There, she could focus on experimenting instead of performing for others. She hoped to go beyond the fluid grace of ballet. Graham hoped to fill her dances with strong feeling and use her body to express emotion.

Graham taught her students different jerky, wobbly, and plunging movements. She used the pumping action of the heart as a guide for creating movement. She taught dancers to tighten and relax the body by breathing. Tightening caved in the stomach while at the same time rounding the back. Relaxing loosened the body and straightened the spine. These new ways to use energy freed the dancers she taught. They used her techniques to stir up emotion.

Like other modern artists, Graham focused her performances on just the basics. She did not use ornate props, sets, or costumes. She used bare stages and lighting, and wore simple dresses. She focused on the movements instead of showiness. She wanted her strong movement to express as much as the music she danced to.

Graham herself was a strong force. In 1936, she refused a request to go to the Olympic Games in Berlin, Germany. At that time, the Nazi party was in power. Many artists in that country had been treated cruelly and unfairly. Graham did not want to be linked with a political power that treated people that way.

Graham did not begin creating her dances with people or ideas, she started with movement. She used dynamic motion to express herself. Some critics thought Graham's dances were offensive. Her brand of modern art shocked some. But Graham believed artistic change could turn into social change. Her dances fill art with new energy.

Today, Martha Graham's dance company still performs many of her 181 dances. She hoped to be remembered as a dancer rather than a choreographer. She felt that her heart belonged to being on center stage. But in truth, she succeeded in both art forms. To this day, critics compare her gift to that of important modern artists like Pablo Picasso.